PUBLISHED BY:

TRUTH AND SOCIAL PUBLICATION

WEBSITE: www.tspublication.com

Raah: A new path towards identity

1st Edition

Price: INR 365/-

ISBN: 978-93-49262-83-6

Dedication

To each person who started their journey with a heart full of hope and a face full of fear. To the unseen give-ups, the nights without sleep, and the belief that tomorrow will be nicer. This book belongs to you and the heritage you bear from one country to another.

"We must accept finite disappointment, but never lose infinite hope."

- Martin Luther King, Jr.

Because migration is not only about movement but it is about memory, belonging, and return.

Varun Singh

Acknowledgements

I bow in thanks to God, whose kindness was the main factor in every step of this journey.

I love my parents the most, whose teachings became the guiding principle I use in every decision. Their intercessions are the secret foundation of my success.

I express my appreciation to my instructors, mentors, and colleagues; the path you provided turned uncertainty into clarity.

To each migrant, student, and family who opened up their story to me, it was you who made this book come alive.

Gratitude

I express my gratitude to the difficult times that showed me how to be strong, to the mistakes that made me careful, and to every person who encouraged me through their silence.

“No matter how much falls on us, we keep plowing ahead. That's the only way to keep the roads clear.” - Greg Kincaid

To the teams who worked beyond the bureaucracy and procedures, my appreciation goes to you for bringing the moral principles into places where shortcuts attempted to thrive.

To my audience, my deepest appreciation goes to you for preferring consciousness over presumption.

Author's Note

Not only is migration a subject of politics, but also a main factor that determines the course of the human race.

The reason I composed this book is to uncover the dark places, shed light on the structures, and safeguard the aspirations that are carried away from home by scared individuals.

The journey of a thousand miles begins with a single step."
- Lao Tzu"

Penny Reid, Truth or Beard

Some people do get lost because they have been given wrong information, and, in the end, they are not the same as before.

This is my reply to the suffering, a pattern that is based on legality, ethics, complete openness, and protection of identity.

If these words make it possible for one family to come forward without fear, that would be the end of their purpose.

Preface

Migration has been the driving force behind the forming and breaking of empires, economies, and even life itself. But every number has its story and every story a heart.

A mother at the door waiting for her child. A father who places his confidence in a stranger's word. A child who becomes an adult in silence and without papers or a past.

The systems that were broken conspired against me and I saw how they dehumanised the people. I saw how the lack of documentation caused people to lose their identities. I saw how lies ruined people's lives.

So, I came up with a new concept, not for movement, but for dignified movement.

history becomes context,

law becomes protection,

and dreams become structured, safe, and real.

These lines of Emma Lazarus's sonnet show about the emotions of migration:

With silent lips. "Give me your tired, your poor,

Your huddled masses yearning to breathe free,

The wretched refuse of your teeming shore.

Send these, the homeless, tempest-tost to me,

I lift my lamp beside the golden door!"

Migration should not be a punishment for those who are ambitious. It should be a reward for the brave.

Turn the page. Walk with clarity.

This book does not tell you to leave your home; it tells you that you can arrive at your future completely.

Contents

Introduction

It was still raining drop by drop but he had to leave. Mohit, the only son of his family, was waiting for the single bus that would take him to the city, which would make his dreams come true and give three course meals for his family. A small bag carrying a million dreams and a few documents, a number saved with "Job wala" someone's cousin had recommended, and a heart full of belief that things would be better on the other side.

His mother's hands didn't want to let him go, and eyes saying the words her lips wouldn't "Beta, come back safe."

Mohit wasn't aware but the advice given to him was false, the hopes were soon going to be shattered. The path ahead was very tough. He was going to be caught in paperwork traps that could crush years of hope in a single rejection stamp.

This is not the migration story of Mohit but most of the people who leave their place with hope but get risks, heartbreak, and silent moments when a dream feels too far away to reach.

Migration

For some, it's the promise of opportunity, a chance to work in a place where their skills are valued and rewarded. For others, it's the pull of safety, the hope of a home far from conflict or instability. And for many, it's the vision of a brighter future for their children.

But between the dream and the destination lies a road that has no destination of security and certainty.

Stories travel faster than facts. Rumors, half-truths, and false promises are lying like the trees in the roads.

And yet, there's another side to this story. One where the road is lit, the milestones clear, and the dream remains the same from start to finish. That's the journey that I have built, not with shortcuts or false guarantees, but with legality, ethics, and a vision for lasting success.

For years, we have been the hand guiding thousands like Mohit, turning fear into clarity, confusion into a plan, and uncertainty into a future.

I am working to make the lines of the poem "Wings of Change" come true,

---

"With feathers light, they break the chain,

In the migration's dance, they find no pain.

Through endless blue, they soar so high,

A quest for life beneath the open sky."

In the pages of this book, you'll find stories not only about migration but about transformation. These are the stories of people who got what they dreamt of; a future where opportunity, safety, and dignity live side by side.

Because migration isn't just a change in geography, it's a change in destiny.

And when you turn the last page, you'll see that migration is not just about moving from one place to another, it's about moving from uncertainty to possibility.

Chapter 1

Roots of Migration - Why People Migrate

Migration hasn't been happening only for a few days, it has existed since the time humans have. The stones have stories of migration carved into them. People have left their homes in search of land, work, safety, or simply hope. Time has changed, but the emotions are the same. In the book of human history migration remains an important chapter. From the journeys of those who settled first to the struggles that colonial labourers faced, from movements during war to today's global migrations, every wave of movement carries the highs and lows, the sacrifices and hopes, and the often untold stories of those who left everything behind to begin again. When we look at the Indian landscape, the story becomes more interesting, how the Indian workers sent to Mauritius, Fiji, and South Africa faced harsh conditions and the situation of India after Partition, when millions left their homes in search of good food and life.

Migration is more than just a journey from one place to another; it's a deeply human story. It's the silent grief of a man who walked away from his family, the unraveling of bonds as he built a new life in a foreign land, leaving behind his past. It's the quiet suffering of children stripped of names, of roots, of a sense of belonging, identities fading with the footsteps of those who never returned.

These lines from poem of Keki Daruwalla represent how migration has been an important part of history

"Migrations are always difficult:

ask any drought,

any plague;

ask the year 1947.

Ask the chronicles themselves:

if there had been no migrations

would there have been enough

history to munch on?"

This chapter will describe migration in the past and the modern factors that encourage migration.

Historical context: Migration from Colonial India to Mauritius, Fiji, South Africa. Partition and Post-Independence Displacement

The past of migration in India isn't written with blood or battle but it is written with fake promises and ink.

The ink which let the people sign a piece of paper to make their dream come true and in return they got nothing but sadness.

- A piece of paper.
- A signature.

- And a dream.

And all this shattered due to the consequences of migration.

In the villages of northern India, where drought cracked the earth, people hoped for nothing but food. Some strange men began to arrive. Agents with sugar coated lies clothed in English silk. They told about the lands across sea, and showed the fake scenario of showering of coins and overflowing of food. This gave hope in the teary eyes of Indians and they thought that five years of work there could buy a life of comfort for their families.

For the poor farmer, the weaver, the widow, and the orphan, the offer was irresistible. It wasn't slavery, they were told it was

- an agreement
- an opportunity
- a deal made with the British Crown itself

But no one knew the truth. This was the start of the Girmitiya System, named after the way Indian tongues twisted the word "agreement" into something softer "girmit". The men and women who signed these contracts would become Girmitiyas indentured labourers shipped across oceans to work in sugar fields, coconut plantations, and rice farms from Mauritius to Fiji, Guyana to Trinidad.

By 1838, over 25,000 Indians had already been packed into ships, sent off with barely more than a sack of grain and the fading memory of home. Over the next eighty years, 1.6 million souls would follow.

When slavery was abolished, colonial plantations across the world stood still. The lands of the empire from the Caribbean to the Pacific needed workers, and fast. But no one was willing to work for free anymore.

So, the British turned to India.

They crafted a new scheme, onc that looked legal and attractive. The contract they brought was neat and clean that included five years of labour, eight rupees a month, food, shelter, and a ticket back home.

But reality was very different!

The white picture had a black shadow!

Agents were paid for every recruit, and their pockets grew fat with each lie they told. The contracts, written in English, weren't understood by the illiterates. The thumb mark took all their rights. Court officers nodded through formalities, pretending to witness consent. Those signing had no idea that they had sold their freedom with just a mark.

To reach the ports at Calcutta or Madras, many Girmitiyas walked for days. Some came barefoot. Some with babies tied to their backs. All came with nothing to lose.

The ships were packed tightly. There were no cabins, just dark holds where hundreds were stacked like grains in a sack. Sanitation was nonexistent. Illness spreads faster than hope. Cholera, dysentery, and starvation claimed many before they even touched foreign soil. Those who survived stepped ashore into lands that would never feel like home.

The plantations of Mauritius, Suriname, and Fiji did not care for promises. They weren't even given the basic services. The Girmitiyas were given huts of mud and wages that barely fed them. Their backs bent in sugar fields. Their hands got blisters due to the burning sun.

The promises were just lies.

- They were told they would be paid. Sometimes they were. Often they were not.
- They were told they could return after five years. Most never did.

The culture changed, Girmitiyas wanted their culture not to be forgotten, so some sang Bhojpuri lullabies to coconut trees. They grew tulsi in the soil of Fiji, Caribbean, and Mauritius. They celebrated Holi with colours made from crushed berries. And slowly, what was Indian became Indo-Fijian, Indo-Caribbean, Indo-Mauritian, a culture born of pain.

Even after the ending of their contracts, returning home wasn't an easy task. If a Girmitiya didn't claim their right to return within six months, it was considered null. Some weren't even told about that. Others were offered small plots of land if they stayed. Many were simply ignored.

And so they have no option left rather than staying.

Sometimes they brought the family over, sometimes they started anew. Some faded into fields they never chose to call home.

Today, their descendants run parliaments and newspapers.

They cook recipes older than the soil beneath their feet.

They dance to the music that echoes to the oceans.

But the legacy of the Girmitiyas isn't just cultural, it's emotional. It's a scar hidden behind the surnames and skin tones.

It is a reminder that colonialism didn't always wear chains. Sometimes, it wore the mask of choice.

The partition of India in 1947

Another major reason behind a huge migration in India was partition. The pain of partition left a lot of people in pain. This migration triggered one of the largest and most tragic mass migrations in human history. Around 15 million people Hindus, Muslims, and Sikhs were forced to leave their homes and cross newly drawn borders in search of safety.

The division of provinces like Punjab and Bengal where different religious communities had lived side by side caused deep chaos. Entire villages were split by borders, and many people didn't even realize what partition meant until they were caught in the middle of it.

Refugees travelled in massive columns, on foot or by overcrowded trains and buses, often becoming targets of brutal attacks. Trains carrying migrants were ambushed, and refugee caravans were attacked. Violence spread rapidly, and according to estimates almost 2 million people were killed in the communal massacres that followed.

The scars of this violent migration lasted for years. The wars, communal conflicts, and refugee crises. It not only shaped the borders of nations but also deeply affected the lives, memories, and identities of millions across generations.

Emotions Behind Migration

Migration is a wound that never gets cured. The families who have suffered are the ones who know the pain. There are kids without names, and have no identity. The borders once crossed by families don't have any returning lines. And these leave tears and pain in the families.

- Who is responsible for the pain of that family?

- Who will be the support of the wife which he left?
- Who will be the feeder of those kids whom he abandons?

Migration has left a lot of questions like this which is sufficient to make your heart shiver. There is personal pain behind the numbers of migration. Behind every migration statistic lies a human story,

The father boarded a flight to the Gulf with dreams in his eyes and promises on his lips, a better future, he said. But the letters stopped, the calls faded, and seasons passed. Somewhere, he planted new roots, started over, and never looked back leaving behind a family suspended in time, waiting for a return that never came. The family lost its caretaker due to migration. The eyes of some parents are still waiting to see their son who left with a promise to bring money to sow the seeds, make the home beautiful and support them till their last breath.

Children of such vanished migrants grow up like shadows, without documents, without names, without a place in the world. They exist between borders and memories, denied identity, denied belonging. Nameless, they carry the silence of abandonment like an inheritance, growing up in the void where a father's promise once lived.

The pain of losing someone's identity is beyond imagination. Imagine living without any name, without the Aadhar card, the Pan card, licence or anything that defines that you are "you".

A good quote I read somewhere says:

"No death, no doom, no anguish can arouse the surpassing despair which flows from a loss of identity."

So imagine how painful it would have been for the children of migrants who lost their identities.

The most deadly experiences which affect the children's mental health are experiences such as discrimination, loss of access to governmental and educational resources, pre-migration trauma, loss of community, cultural distance and acculturation, the burden on the family unit, and socioeconomic difficulties.

Migration is not only about the geographical changes or crossing the boundaries; it is a transformation of identity, a reshaping of values, and often, a painful severance from the familiar. It may bring money or food on one hand but it leaves behind deep cultural imprints, some nurturing, others distressing.

The migration process unfolds in three broad stages: pre-migration, migration, and post-migration. Each stage carries its own cultural effects. During pre-migration, individuals start detaching from familiar norms while carrying hopes, expectations, and sometimes trauma from persecution or forced displacement. Migration, the physical act of relocating, often includes culture shock, disorientation, and the early signs of identity conflict. In the post-migration phase, migrants encounter the most complex cultural challenges: assimilation, social acceptance, language barriers, and role redefinition in families and communities.

What has begun as the dream for a better future, now slowly reveals itself as a trade-off where the past becomes both a memory and a burden.

Social roles learned over generations change. Gender dynamics shift. Parenting styles evolve. Rituals lose their original form. For many, the struggle is not just about fitting into a new world, but about not losing themselves in the process.

Migration has different psychological effects and the one that is often overlooked is cultural bereavement, the grief that comes from losing one's social structure, traditions, and way of life. This experience isn't only about the nostalgic feeling of one's culture but it includes guilt over leaving one's homeland, pain when cultural memories fade, and even some harmful thoughts of ancestral spirits or unresolved cultural obligations. For many migrants, this unspoken grief has become a part of their daily life, sometimes misdiagnosed as depression or anxiety due to a lack of cultural understanding in the host country's healthcare system.

For example, a migrant may feel "out of place" in a society where their language, food, clothing, or belief systems are treated as alien or inferior. Over time, these exclusions combine and get reformed into isolation, self-doubt, and a fractured identity especially when migrants are not accepted by the dominant culture and also feel distanced from their own communities.

> *"I am from there. I am from here. I am not there and I am not here. I have two names which meet and part, and I have two languages, I forget which one I dream in."*
>
> *Mahmoud Darwish,*
> *Palestinian poet.*

This quote resonates perfectly with the pain of losing one's own culture by migration.

The challenge of acculturation means adapting to a new culture while preserving one's original identity varies from person to person. Migrants find themselves disoriented in individualistic societies and this creates inner tension, role confusion, and often a generational divide between parents and children raised in different cultural frameworks.

Moreover, the degree of cultural similarity or dissimilarity between the origin and settlement country influences this process. A migrant from a culturally aligned nation may experience smoother integration, while those from vastly different backgrounds may face discrimination, language barriers, and cultural alienation.

Modern Migration Drivers

Migration today is not just about crossing borders.

It is about crossing boundaries of despair to reach toward dignity. It is not only about leaving something behind, it is about building something new.

A home. A future. A name.

In every train that departs from the heartlands of Bihar, Uttar Pradesh, Odisha, Jharkhand, or Bengal.

In every bus that carries families wrapped in plastic sheets and trembling hope. There is a story that often goes unseen.

- A father clutching a steel tiffin, leaving his children asleep to board a train at 3 AM.
- A mother holding her child on her lap, dreaming of a city where her daughter might one day go to school.
- A boy who speaks fluent Bhojpuri and broken Hindi but believes he can learn English if given a chance.

They are not running away. They are reaching out.

While the reasons for migration have evolved over time, the modern migrant often stands at the intersection of compulsion and ambition. On one side lies poverty, unemployment, and widening economic inequality. On the other, the hunger for education, safety, healthcare, and a better future. Migration today is not merely about escaping, it is about arriving, building, and leaving something better behind.

Pushed by Hardship

At its core, migration in India, especially internal migration, is often triggered by economic distress. Entire families leave their native villages due to shrinking agricultural opportunities, failing monsoons, landlessness, and lack of industrial development in rural belts. Youths leave small towns where education ends at the 10th standard and jobs are few and far between.

In megacities, they become construction workers, delivery agents, domestic help, or factory labourers, essential to the urban economy, yet excluded from its benefits. The informal nature of their employment means there is no job security, no insurance, and no safety net.

Pulled by Dreams

Yet migration is not solely a tale of desperation, it is equally a story of desire.

Many migrate not just to survive, but to thrive. They seek better schools for their children, access to reliable healthcare, and freedom from caste-based hierarchies or communal tensions. They chase dignity, not just employment.

For women, migration can mean liberation from patriarchal control. For youth, it is a ticket to opportunity. For families, it is a calculated risk taken with one goal: a better life for the next generation.

- There is poverty, the kind that soars at pride.
- There is unemployment, where skill meets silence.
- There is inequality, so deep that the distance between two cities can feel like two centuries.

But just as real is the pull,

- The pull of a better life.
- A school that teaches more than survival.
- A hospital that doesn't turn away the poor.
- A job that brings money, and maybe a little dignity too.
- A life where their children will not sleep hungry or grow up invisible.

Migration as Legacy-Building

What is often forgotten in policy discussions is that migrants are not just workers, they are visionaries in motion. Every remittance they send, every sacrifice they make, is a brick in the legacy they are trying to build.

But legacy cannot be built on fragile ground. When migrants live without documentation, legal protection, housing rights, or access to education and healthcare, their journey toward a better life becomes one of exploitation and erasure.

Rewriting the Migration Story: My Vision for Change

Recognizing the patterns etched into both history and the headlines of today, I found myself asking: Has anything truly changed? From the Girmitiyas who signed with hope but sailed into hardship, to the children of modern migrants growing up without names or rights, the thread was painfully familiar. Migration, for too long, has been a response to desperation, not a pursuit of dignity.

I could no longer remain a passive observer to this generational pain. I knew that we needed more than just stories, we needed a system that understood the human behind the movement.

Migration is a Letter to the Future

When a man leaves his village, he does not just carry a bag of clothes.

- He carries the weight of generations and the hope of the next.
- He becomes invisible in cities. He wears uniforms without names.
- He works behind your walls, beneath your feet, under your cars.
- You don't see him, but your life stands on his shoulders.

And yet, he dreams.

- He dreams that one day, his son won't lay bricks, he will build companies.
- That his daughter won't sweep homes, she'll own one.
- This is the quiet legacy of a migrant.

- He builds not just roads and buildings, but futures.

But legacy needs recognition.

Too often, migrants live without names. Without ration cards, voter IDs, school admission, healthcare, or even a permanent address. They are punished for their movement. Denied rights because they dared to move. Their children grow up without certificates, sometimes without surnames, as if the system itself forgets they exist. We speak of GDP and development, of smart cities and digital India. **But what about the people who build them?**

- India runs on the feet of its workers.
- It is they who dig the roads, build the bridges, cook your food, and sweep your malls.
- And yet, their own dreams often collapse under the weight of bureaucracy, neglect, and exclusion.

They need a model that does not punish ambition or survival, but honour them. That's when I began working on an immigration framework that would do more than manage movement; it would transform it.

This wasn't just about opening borders, it was about opening pathways. I envisioned a system that addressed the root causes: poverty, unemployment, educational inequality, gendered violence, and lack of access to healthcare. These are not isolated issues, they are the quiet forces that push people to leave everything behind.

So, I set out to design an immigration model that is structured, legal, and deeply personal. A model that gives migrants a roadmap, not a dead end. That replaces confusion with clarity, fear with safety, and silence with voice.

In this vision, migration becomes a choice, not a last resort. It becomes a tool for legacy-building, not just survival. And at the core of this vision is a simple belief: no human being should lose their identity in the process of finding a better life.

This model isn't just a policy proposal, it's my personal response to the cries I've heard in archives, in refugee camps, and in my own memory. It's my commitment to make sure that history's wounds don't remain open scars. It's a promise that the next chapter of migration will be one of dignity, documentation, and dreams fulfilled not abandoned.

Chapter 2

Identity in Crisis - When Systems Fail

Imagine waking up one day to find your name misspelled, your fingerprint unrecognizable, and the world insisting you are someone you are not. That is the quiet violence millions endure. It's a rough stretch of life where old assumptions feel foreign, long-held ideals slip from your understanding, and the version of yourself you thought you knew demands a second look.

When systems fail, it affects individual identity, and it can bring major life changes, or the ripple effects of others' activities are most commonly experienced during the volatile years of adolescence and early adulthood. It is a forced break to tear apart and rebuild who you truly are.

It is a result of losing a valued role, encountering repeated failures, or experiencing prolonged periods of instability. This failure can ruin one's self-confidence, forcing a re-evaluation of their abilities and future, yet creating a deep-seated discomfort and uncertainty about who they are.

One afternoon in Bengal, we stumbled across a rally of migrant workers. Their voices carried anger and exhaustion, but also fear. Later, I heard how police had pulled men straight from worksites, men who had done nothing wrong, and locked them away for weeks. Their only crime was a typo on a document, a stamp missing from a page, or a birth date that didn't line up with an old register.

I still remember one man's face as he described leaving his children behind to earn money in another state, only to be treated like a criminal. He worked long hours so his family wouldn't go hungry, sending wages home rupee by rupee. Yet, because some file somewhere didn't "recognise" him, the system acted as if he didn't exist. His fear was real. His anger made sense. And for the first time, I saw just how fragile identity can become when systems fail.

What we saw in West Bengal was not an isolated injustice. Across India, the same cracks in documentation systems were tearing lives apart, in villages, ration shops, and even voting booths.

It was an injustice, and the injustice didn't end with wrongful custody. In Meghalaya, factories quietly sheltered undocumented migrants who also provided them cover, while elsewhere, workers with valid records were being arrested. The system punished some while protecting others by proving just how inconsistent and fragile these tools really were.

If identity can be questioned selectively, is it really about the law or just about who happens to have the right stamp at the right time?

I remember speaking to a man who whispered, ***"When they questioned my papers, it felt like they were questioning my right to exist in the only land I've ever known."***

Many didn't even know which office could solve their problem. Our mission was to work for justice and prevent wrongful custody. In Odisha, mobile migrant help centres were launched to help workers secure documents on the move. We have also worked alongside similar initiatives which ensure these programs are not just announcements on paper but lifelines for real people.

We have stood shoulder to shoulder with administrators willing to listen, making bridges between governments, police stations, and migrant communities. Actually, our goal was simple: to make sure no man, woman, or child is stripped of their presence because a form wasn't filled out accurately.

Every time I meet a worker whose life has been torn apart by a missing document, I ask myself a question:

- How can a single sheet of paper decide a person's worth?
- Why should a minor error cost someone their home, their job, or their family?

These are not just paperwork problems. They are human crises. They tear families apart, rob people of their dignity, and leave them wandering in a no-man's land where they belong nowhere.

"Unlike a drop of water which loses its identity when it joins the ocean, man does not lose his being in the society in which he lives."

- B. R. Ambedkar

In this chapter, I will share these stories not to point fingers, but to tell the truth: when documentation systems fail, people vanish. Their voices go unheard. Their faces become files stamped "pending." And in those points, it falls to us, those who care enough to fight, to bring them back into view.

My team and I have discovered that restoring documentation integrity is not just about bureaucracy. It is about humanity. It is about glimpsing a person in the eye and saying, "You are not invisible. We will not allow the system to forget who you are."

Whether we were racing against deadlines to stop wrongful arrests or guiding families through the maze of paperwork, our mission was always the same: to prove something that should never be in doubt: a person's identity.

- This is the confusion I have seen.
- This is the problem of identity.
- And this is the fight we continue to fight to ensure that no one is erased by a clerical mistake, a missing stamp, or a system too rigid to visit the human being behind the document.

Real-world consequences of flawed documentation systems.

Identity papers are not just paper and numbers; they imply a person and basic rights, dignity, and belonging. When these strategies break, the fallout can be deeply human and painfully tangible.

And what we saw on the ground matched stories reported elsewhere. These failures weren't just about migrants, they cut across age, geography, and class

When the System Fails the Elderly

I read a story about an identity crisis which happened due to a system failure. Sumanto Hembrom, an 80-year-old widow from Jharkhand, stood in the ration line with the same hands that had carried firewood, cooked for her children, and tilled the soil for decades. Yet the machine at the counter could not recognize those hands. Her fingerprints, worn down by a lifetime of labor, failed to match the Aadhaar database. For months, she went without her food rations.

"The hunger was not the worst part," she whispered once, "it was standing in front of others and being told by a screen that I do not exist."

Her story is not an exception; it is a mirror. Across India, millions stand before that same cold mirror every day, watching their reflection blur because of a spelling mistake, a failed biometric scan, or a missing piece of paper.

In West Bengal, during the tense run-up to elections, questions over citizenship erupted into fear and violence. One man told me quietly, "When they doubted my papers, it felt like they doubted my right to belong to the only land I have ever known."

For the elderly, whose fingerprints fade like their eyesight, the system becomes a wall. For migrant workers carrying torn documents across states, every checkpoint feels like a trial. And for those who suffer identity fraud, the betrayal is not only financial but deeply human technology turning against the very people it was built to serve.

These are not clerical errors. They are wounds. And behind each failed verification lies a life slowly erased.

Confusion and Chaos: When Aadhaar Loses Its Edge

In Delhi, Bihar migrant workers faced growing uncertainty when the Election Commission began its Special Intensive Revision (SIR) of the voter list. They used to rely on Aadhaar as their golden ticket for paperwork, but now, it "has lost its edge." Many submitted their Aadhaar, sceptical about what to expect next or whether it would even help.

Surveys found that 75% of Bihar migrants were unaware of the SIR portal or basic enrollment requirements, and most lacked a clear report on what documents were required. This confusion is not bureaucratic; it is deeply personal. It puts livelihoods, voices, and democratic rights on the line.

When Identity Becomes a Tool for Deception

As identity papers stutter, some turn to fraud and the consequences ripple far beyond the scam. In Surat, two brothers from Bihar faced arrest after police discovered they had created fake Aadhaar cards with changed religious identities only so they could see lodging and jobs more easily.

Meanwhile, in Lucknow's Kushinagar district, a gang was dismantled for selling fake birth certificates and Aadhaar cards, trapping countless unsuspecting people in a web of lies. And in a shocking bust, the UP Anti-Terrorism Squad revealed a sprawling interstate noise that produced forged Aadhaar cards and identity records for Rohingyas, Bangladeshis, Nepalis, and other undocumented immigrants.

Real-World Implications for Migrants and Citizens

Migration impacts migrants through potential revenue increases but also vulnerability to trauma and human rights violations. It impacts citizens by filling labour shortages and contributing to demographic balance. But it also potentially increases cost-of-living problems and competition for resources. Flawed documentation systems have real, human consequences that go far beyond paperwork.

- **Benefit Denial:** When biometric authentication fails due to worn fingerprints, old age, or technical glitches, people are locked out of basic welfare plans. Such errors delay everything, from school admissions to salary disbursals.
- **Identity Disputes:** A small spelling mistake or mismatched date of birth can snowball into an identity problem. Such errors delay everything from school admissions for children to salary disbursals for employees. What should be a simple correction becomes a long, stressful battle to "prove" one's own existence.
- **Legal and Economic Vulnerability:** Fake or incorrect documentation creates options for exploitation. Unscrupulous middlemen sell generated IDs, trapping unsuspecting individuals in criminal networks. Workers without proper documents risk wrongful arrest, eviction from rented rooms, or even deportation, while genuine residents get involved in verification drives.
- **Policy Confusion & Distrust:** Inconsistent use of Aadhaar deepens distrust. Migrants who depend on it to prove their legality suddenly find it questioned or insufficient. When policies shift without clear communication, entire communities are left confused, unsure how to access fundamental services or protect their rights.

These issues show that documentation errors are not just technical faults; they are human crises. They strip people of pride, stability, and safety, demonstrating that identity systems must be designed and executed with compassion, clarity, and fairness.

Why These Cases Matter

- **Criminalising Authentic Citizens:** Most of those excluded are not criminals, they are simply victims of a rigid system that fails to see them.
- **Democracy Hanging by a Thread:** Again, when migrants do not know how to use Aadhaar or its relevance shifts overnight, it leaves their political rights in limbo.
- **Erosion of Trust & Rise of Illicit Networks:** When real documentation fails or costs too much, it opens the door to criminal profiteers for innocent people and creates a parallel identity underworld.
- **Widening Inequality:** Those with the key to understanding, tech, or options benefit. Those without, such as the elderly, poor, or migrant workers, fall further behind.
- **Documentation Integrity:** As human beings, our identity depends on documents and from birth to death, people's identity is recognised by their documents. So it is the backbone of identity, legality, and trust. If their documents have any mistakes or the system fails in record-keeping, it can destroy lives. In this incident, we had seen in cases of migrants, elderly citizens, or marginalized groups denied their rights because a document was misspelled, missing, or mismatched.

So the question remains: if the system is broken, how can it be rebuilt? Outrage and empathy alone are not enough. We need working models that prove documentation can be reliable, humane, and transparent. One such model we've seen in action is our model.

For more than 15 years, I have worked with a 100% paperless documentation system. Unlike traditional methods, where files move physically across desks and are prone to misplacement, loss, or tampering, I digitised the entire process.

This digital-first process is controlled through an integrated Customer Relationship Management (CRM) and Enterprise Resource Planning (ERP) platform. Every customer file is documented, tracked, and stored digitally, ensuring that there is no ambiguity about its place, status, or authenticity.

One of the core strengths of this method lies in its multi-layered keeping checks. Each document experiences verification at several stages, which can reduce the likelihood of errors slipping through. For example, where a manual approach might overlook a misspelling or a date mismatch, the system flags these inconsistencies directly. This layered proof creates both accountability and scalability. For example, whether the firm is managing ten clients or ten thousand, the process remains equally robust.

In this scenario, the result is remarkable, such as zero data loss and 100% efficiency. In an era where misplaced files or incorrect entries can have devastating results, from illegal custody of migrants to denial of welfare benefits, the assurance that every record is maintained accurately is not just a technological accomplishment but also a social security. In fact, what makes our system mainly significant is not only its technical backbone but the way it matches human expertise with digital infrastructure. While devices secure accuracy, human oversight ensures context and fairness.

This approach also makes the procedure transparent. Transparency, in this sense, does not just protect the client; it also protects the organisation from allegations of discrimination, negligence, or malpractice. In competitive industries, this kind of reliability becomes a differentiator, and I have built a reputation that many competitors envy but few can replicate.

The broader implication of this model goes beyond corporate efficiency. It shows how documentation integrity can be achieved when organisations are ready to invest in systems that prioritise accuracy, transparency, and scalability. In essence, it's more than a success story; it provides a blueprint. A blueprint where technology and human accountability converge to provide that documentation systems are not only about keeping information but about protecting identity, dignity, and trust.

A Path Forward: Proposals and Hopeful Steps

Civil rights bodies are ringing the alarm bell. They are requesting that alternative authentication methods, such as OTPs, facial recognition, or 'exceptional enrollment' methods, be made the default, not the exception.

Community outreach, awareness campaigns, and local nodal officers are important, mainly in areas where digital literacy or access remains low. Its measures can control exclusion before it is too late to ensure dignity and rights remain intact.

The Human Stories Behind the Numbers

Yet, behind every failed authentication or forged certificate lies a person. Sumanto's empty hands, the migrant worker unsure of his voting rights, or the family misled by false Aadhaar, all of them deserve more than bureaucratic indifference.

Because every person, regardless of age, income, or events, should be able to say: ***"I exist. My identity matters. And***

I won't be ignored." My team has seen firsthand how these situations spiral. When documentation systems fail to account for gender diversity, even small discrepancies, an old photo, a name change, or a mismatch in gender markers can lead to wrongful detention. In some cases, migrants are caught without valid papers; in others, legal citizens are presumed illegal simply because their appearance defies stereotypes. Both groups end up trapped in the same bureaucratic nightmare. The solution cannot be more harassment or blanket suspicion. It must be documentation systems that respect self-identified gender, training for frontline officials to prevent abuse, and strong legal aid for anyone whose identity is questioned.

The Supreme Court's rulings and the 2019 Act give India the tools, but these tools must be put to work in real police stations, border checkpoints, and welfare offices.

And we are working to integrate the documents so that they can have their identity. A name they can call their own officially.

Identity systems must not erase people. They must protect them. Because every person, regardless of age, income, or gender, has the right to identity.

As Amartya Sen says "The identity of an individual is essentially a function of her choices, rather than the discovery of an immutable attribute."

We do not fight for perfect databases. We fight so no Sumanto, no migrant, no forgotten name, disappears into silence. We fight so that when a person looks into the mirror, they see themselves, clear, whole, and unshaken.

Chapter 3
When Dreams Collide with Deception

I have met enough families to know that a suitcase is never just a suitcase. In India, when a child prepares to study abroad, the bag carries more than clothes and books, it carries an entire family's hopes, sacrifices, and quiet prayers.

And yet, alongside every dream runs the shadow of deception. I have seen glossy brochures, slick websites, and confident agents who speak with such certainty that even the most cautious parent begins to believe. To the untrained eye, these promises look legitimate; to desperate families, they feel like the only path forward. Too often, they end in heartbreak.

I still remember the morning I opened a European newspaper with the headline: *"Hundreds of Indian students deported for forged admission letters."* The very next week, Canada reported a similar story. Different countries, same pain. Behind each headline, I did not see "statistics." I saw parents mortgaging ancestral land, mothers parting with the last of their jewelry, siblings whispering prayers into the night. I saw what happens when dreams collide with deception.

Stories like these are not isolated. Across continents, families fall prey to promises that seem too good to be true. Quick visas, guaranteed jobs, and permanent residency, all offered with a smile and a signature on a glossy brochure. And yet, beneath the polished surface lies a reality that can shatter lives overnight.

A Family's Empty Room

One memory will never leave me. In a small Punjab home, a mother placed an empty jewelry box in front of me. She held it not as an object but as proof of sacrifice. Her husband had sold a piece of land their family had owned for generations. With trembling pride, they had told me once, *"For our son, we can give away everything."*

I realized then that it was not carelessness that led them here, but hope, the kind that makes a family mortgage land or part with a cherished possession in pursuit of a brighter future.

But pride turned into silence when they discovered the admission letter was a forgery. Their son returned home in shame. Neighbors whispered. Debt piled up. The father, once so certain, now looked down at the floor and said quietly, *"I thought I was doing it for him. I thought I was doing it for us."*

This heartbreak is not unique. It echoes in countless homes where trust is misplaced, and dreams collide with deception. I sat in that room and felt the weight of their loss. This was not a financial miscalculation. It was heartbreak, a story repeated across cities, villages, and communities, in families who dared to dream of a brighter future.

Misinformation, Mistrust, and the Need for Guidance

How Misinformation Becomes a Trap

Fraud rarely preys on greed alone, it preys on hope. Families make life-altering decisions based on rumors, forwarded WhatsApp messages, or the success story of a neighbor's child. In these gaps, unscrupulous agents weave their lies: "quick visas," "guaranteed jobs," "permanent residency."

I once asked a father in Haryana if he had verified the university's credentials online. He lowered his eyes and admitted, "We only trusted the brochure the agent gave us." It was not laziness or negligence, it was trust, sincere yet misplaced. And once that trust is broken, it leaves wounds that do not heal easily.

One father I spoke to in Haryana admitted: "We never checked the university website. We only believed the brochure the agent gave us. Later, we discovered the institution did not even exist."

This reliance on second-hand sources leads to mistrust in the entire migration process. Even genuine consultancies and verified universities are viewed with suspicion because fraud has poisoned the atmosphere. Hopeful students and workers no longer know whom to believe.

This mistrust has serious consequences. Families delay decisions until it is too late. Students miss application deadlines. Workers lose job opportunities. And in the end, desperation grows making them even easier targets for the very fraudsters they are trying to avoid.

What is missing is guidance that is both accurate and accessible. Migrants do not just need a service; they need someone who will tell them not only what is possible but also what is not. A trustworthy advisor is one who says "no" as often as they say "yes".

Because when misinformation spreads, the cost is not just financial it is emotional, social, and generational. A wrong decision can push a family into debt that lasts for decades. A single forged document can end an entire career before it begins.

Faces of Fraud

Fraud wears many masks. Sometimes it welcomes you in a sleek office, adorned with posters of Big Ben or the Statue of Liberty. Sometimes it hides behind a phone number that changes with every call, a voice that promises miracles.

Take the case of Rakinder, a young man from Punjab who believed he had found a shortcut to the United States. The agent he trusted never revealed his real name, only calling from different numbers and demanding payments in stages. First for "processing," then for "tickets," then for "border arrangements." Rakinder's family sold their land, paying nearly ₹45 lakh. What followed was a dangerous journey through Brazil, a passport stolen by middlemen, nights spent walking through jungles, and finally, deportation. "I walked for weeks, but instead of America, I returned with nothing but shame," he later said.

Students, too, fall prey to carefully woven lies. In 2019, more than a hundred Indian students in the United States were arrested not because they committed a crime, but because they had unknowingly enrolled in a fake university set up to trap migrants. In Canada, over 150 students received deportation letters after officials uncovered forged admission papers. One young woman, Dimple, described the pain simply: "My mind is dark. I cannot move forward, nor go back."

Fraud also reaches into the very foundation of identity. In Uttar Pradesh, a gang was caught creating fake Aadhaar cards, charging anywhere between ₹2,000 and ₹40,000. These forged IDs became the basis for passports, visas, and other official documents. Many who trusted these agents found themselves arrested abroad, punished for crimes they did not even know they were committing.

Across Europe, another scam unfolded when a law firm issued fake embassy letters to hundreds of families. The papers looked real, the stamps official, the signatures convincing. Only later did victims learn that everything was fabricated. Families were left stranded, their savings gone. Yet those guided by strong compliance systems avoided the trap proof that not every path has to end in despair.

Whether through a ghost agent whispering on WhatsApp, a fake university hiding behind a website, or a forged identity card produced in a small-town office, the result is the same: broken dreams, empty homes, and futures rewritten by betrayal.

Consequences - Broken Families, Debt, and Emotional Trauma

When families lose land or jewelry, it is never just money they lose, it is heritage, pride, and security. Fathers may withdraw from village meetings. Mothers may avoid neighbors' eyes. Children may refuse to leave their rooms after deportation.

The real cost is invisible, yet devastating. Financial loss is temporary. The emotional scars, the erosion of dignity, and the quiet weight of shame can last a lifetime.

Behind every fraud is not only greed but also misinformation. Families often make life-changing decisions based on half-truths, rumors, or misleading promises. In small towns, a neighbor's son who "went abroad" becomes the benchmark, and agents exploit this social pressure by painting glossy pictures of quick visas, guaranteed jobs, and permanent residency.

In Punjab and Haryana, it is common for families to sell farmland or ancestral homes to fund a child's migration. For them, sending a son or daughter abroad is not just a choice, it is a matter of pride, a step toward lifting the family into a better future. But when the dream collapses, the pride turns into silence. Fathers stop attending village meetings. Mothers avoid eye contact with neighbors. Relatives whisper: "They were cheated... they lost everything."

Debt is the heaviest chain. Families who borrow at high interest rates from local lenders find themselves unable to repay once the promised job or admission evaporates. The interest compounds, assets are seized, and in some cases, families are forced to work menial jobs just to service loans taken in hope of prosperity.

The emotional toll is even greater. I met a student who returned after being deported from Europe. His father confessed: "He does not leave his room. He feels ashamed to walk in the village. People think he failed, but it was we who failed him."

Mental health struggles depression, anxiety, even suicidal thoughts become common among those who feel they have ruined not only their own life but also the future of their family. The weight of expectation, once a source of motivation, becomes unbearable when dreams collapse.

Families themselves fracture under the strain. Some parents blame children for trusting the wrong agent. Some children blame parents for pressuring them to go abroad at any cost. Marriages are delayed or broken, siblings quarrel over lost property, and entire households carry scars that may never heal.

And yet, perhaps the most tragic consequence is loss of trust. People begin to doubt every opportunity, every document, every word of advice. Even genuine agencies or universities are met with suspicion. The system itself appears corrupt, and hopes once the strongest driver of migration turns into fear.

The Firewall - Ethical Leadership and Protection Against Fraud

In a world where false promises spread like wildfire, what families need is not just opportunity, but protection. Protection from lies, from shortcuts, from the invisible traps that lure people into debt and despair. This is where ethical leadership matters.

I often describe my role as being a firewall. In technology, a firewall protects users from hidden threats. In migration, ethical leadership plays that very role.

I recall a European case where forged embassy letters looked so authentic that hundreds of families were deceived. The stamps seemed official, the signatures convincing. Many lost everything. But the families who had chosen a compliance-driven path were spared. Why? Because every document had been verified, every inconsistency flagged, every too-good-to-be-true promise questioned.

Being a firewall is not glamorous. It means saying "no" when a desperate family longs to hear "yes." It means absorbing their frustration when the process is slower than they wish. It means refusing revenue when something feels wrong.

But the reward is greater than any commission: families protected, futures secured, and trust preserved. Our role is not to sell dreams, it is to safeguard them.

A firewall, in technology, blocks threats before they cause damage. In the migration world, ethical organizations act as that firewall standing between hopeful migrants and the predators who exploit them. We do this not by making bigger promises, but by insisting on compliance, documentation, and accountability.

My team has been more than a consultancy; it has been a fireproof wall shielding clients from failure, fraud, and misrepresentation. We take every burn on behalf of our clients, never letting them suffer damage. This is the difference between working with an unregulated player and an ethics-driven, compliance-certified leader.

Being a firewall is not easy. It means rejecting cases that appear profitable but raise red flags. It means educating families about risks, even if they don't want to hear the truth. It means standing in the line of fire, absorbing the frustration of clients who want instant results, while refusing to compromise on integrity.

But the rewards are powerful. Every family protected from fraud becomes a story of trust. Every student guided safely to a real university rebuilds faith in the system. Every worker placed in a legitimate job proves that migration can still be dignified.

Ethical leadership is not about selling dreamsit is about safeguarding them. By logging every file, tracking every promise, and reporting every suspicious actor, such leadership reshapes the industry itself. ***Fraud thrives in secrecy; accountability shines light into the shadows.***

Over time, this approach transforms despair into resilience. Families who once felt betrayed begin to hope again not blindly, but wisely. They learn that trust does not mean naivety, and opportunity does not have to mean exploitation.

Because ultimately, migration is not just about moving from one country to another. It is about moving from fear to confidence, from uncertainty to dignity. And that journey can only be secured when leaders choose ethics over shortcuts, and accountability over profit.

Rebuilding Trust and Educating Communities

Fraud thrives in silence. Families rarely speak openly about being cheated, fearing humiliation in their communities. This silence allows ghost agents and fake consultancies to survive, moving from one victim to the next. Breaking this cycle requires more than individual protection, it demands education and collective awareness.

This is where our team has gone beyond being a consultancy and stepped into the role of a community educator. Over the years, the team has launched awareness campaigns, client education sessions, and transparent documentation practices designed to protect not only those who sign up with our team, but also those who may never become clients.

During community sessions in smaller towns, I witnessed how parents asked the most basic yet crucial questions:

- "How do I know if a university is real?"
- "What happens if the visa gets rejected?"
- "How can we verify an agent's credentials?"

Our team does not dismiss these questions. Instead, we patiently break down the process, showing official portals, explaining red flags, and even teaching families how to do basic verification themselves. By empowering people with knowledge, we reduce the power of fraudsters.

A recent awareness drive in northern India drew hundreds of families. Many admitted they had already been approached by unregistered agents. One father said afterwards: "For the first time, I understood that saying no to an agent is also a way of protecting my son."

This educational role has another ripple effect: it rebuilds trust. When people see that our team is willing to say "this case cannot be processed" or "this route is illegal," we begin to realize that honesty is itself a form of service. Clients no longer see transparency as a delay, but as a safeguard.

By reporting fraudulent practices, refusing shortcuts, and shining a light on risks, our team has helped clean parts of the ecosystem that had been poisoned by deception. Families who once hesitated now approach the company not just for paperwork, but for clarity. They come seeking truth, not merely opportunity.

In this way, our team is reshaping the industry's reputation. Migration no longer has to mean danger or deceit. With accountability at its core, the company has shown that it is possible to dream without being destroyed, and to hope without being exploited.

Protecting the Dignity of Migration

In the end, migration is not just about visas, approvals, or paperwork it is about dignity. Every individual who dares to step into a new country carries a story, a sacrifice, and a dream. What destroys these dreams is not the difficulty of the process, but the betrayal of trust.

This is why my team is not merely a consultancy, it is a commitment. A commitment that no client should feel alone, cheated, or misled. A promise that even if the answer is "not possible," it will be said with honesty and compassion.

For countless families, our team has become the voice of reassurance when fear dominates, the hand of guidance when confusion overwhelms, and the shield of protection when fraud lurks in the shadows. It is not about selling an opportunity; it is about safeguarding the right to dream.

Migration should never feel like a gamble. With us, it becomes a journey of clarity where every step is verified, every process transparent, and every decision backed by truth.

As one client said after completing their long-awaited relocation: "*Others took our money. But this team gave us back our faith.*"

That is the real measure of success. Not the number of visas processed, but the number of lives protected. Not the documents filed, but the dignity preserved.

And as the world continues to change, one thing remains constant: *We will always stand as a guardrail against deception, a defender of integrity, and a builder of trust.*

Because in the story of migration, the most powerful passport is not stamped by an embassy it is stamped by trust.

Chapter 4
The Legal Lifeline

Migration is not only about crossing borders, it is about navigating a web of laws and protections. Without this legal lifeline, even the brightest dream can collapse; with it, families can walk their journey with confidence.

The legal lifeline refers to the laws, policies, and organizations that protect migrants and ensure their rights. It is important for those people who are thinking of going abroad, in one word, we can say for migrant people. It can provide legal support and protection to migrants. How can migrants benefit from the legal lifeline? Without this legal safety net, migrants are vulnerable to exploitation, denial of services, and social exclusion. It also provides access to justice and basic services, often through legal awareness programs, community support, and assistance in obtaining legal identity documents.

When you see your friends, relatives, or neighbours are settled abroad or traveled in foreign country. What do you think? Is it easy to go? No, before entering any country, they have encountered many legal barriers. First of all, migrant workers lie on the legal lifeline. The main reason is social security, protection against exploitation. It also helps to access the basic rights and assist during their crisis to overcome those situations. But the legal frameworks and government schemes provide important assistance to the migrants to combat their difficult situation. Sometimes, they lack documents, have poor awareness regarding the law and rights related to migration, administrative neglect, and insufficient enforcement.

I once met a father from Haryana who told me, 'We never knew we had the right to question an agent. We thought whatever he said was the law.' That moment reminded me that legal literacy is just as important as legal compliance.

According to Aristotle

"The law is reason, free from passion."

I have read a case study of Delhi from 2011, which reported that around 43.03% of its population were migrants. The migrant workers in Delhi faced many challenges, such as inadequate housing, low pay, discrimination based on class/caste/gender, poor housing, social protection schemes, and disruption in the schooling of children. The COVID-19 lockdown further worsened these challenges, exposing the fragility of migrant protections.

The pandemic showed us that without strong legal frameworks, migrants stand on shifting ground, one crisis is enough to uproot their lives.

On the other hand, in 2019, as part of its labour law reform initiative in India, it started the exercise of consolidating 29 central labour laws into four major labour codes. However, many fear that these reforms may dilute existing protections and entitlements.

Legal migration as a tool of dignity and protection

When you think of going abroad for a job, education or travelling. It is not easy to move from one country to another. You have to go through a lot of laws and regulations. To follow the lengthy process, you can be annoyed and frustrated. You have a dream, do not give up, because this legal process is lengthy, but it can give you a smooth journey without barriers to entering another country.

Migration plays an important role. It can change individual lives. It can change the social, economic, and cultural aspects of the world. When you think of settling abroad, you must understand the legal process. If you miss anything, it can bring unexpected disturbance. If you follow the legal migration process, it can keep human dignity and protection rather than it can prevent exploitation and vulnerability. Jorge Ramos said, **"The greatest nations are defined by how they treat their weakest inhabitants."**

Legal migration is a powerful tool. It involves shifting from one nation to another by obeying the legal rules and regulations of both nations. It contains appropriate visas, work permits, papers, residency documents, etc. This process is difficult. Sometimes it can induce a crisis. But after completing this process, you can go abroad smoothly without any legal trouble. Countries like Canada, Germany, and Australia actively promote legal migration channels to ensure fairness and skill mobility. If you are an Indian worker, it is essential in the Gulf countries that the legal channels ensure fair agreements, which control recruitment and provide access to grievance redressal tools. In contrast, if you do not follow this legal procedure, it can pose a threat to your journey. Even if you somehow work to reach it, you might face legal issues at some point. Again, you can often fall prey to dishonest agents who exploit working conditions or human trafficking. To avoid these issues, you can follow the legal migrant process. It can help you to get access to healthcare, social security advantages, and labour rights. It can help to keep your dignity as human beings by reducing you to "irregular" or "undocumented" labour.

Irregular migration may look like a shortcut, but it often ends in detention, deportation, or lifelong bans. In contrast, legal migration, though slower, builds dignity and permanent protection.

The importance of legal migration contributes to India as a trustworthy global player. If you follow this legal migration procedure, you can take multiple benefits. You can work in foreign country safely without any legal barriers, which are mainly faced by other immigrants who have no valid documents.

According to the United Nations Sustainable Development Goal (SDG) 10.7, it promotes orderly, safe, stable, and responsible migration and mobility of people. It includes the performance of planned and well-managed migration procedures. It also promotes better skill mobility, and the Pravasi Kaushal Vikas Yojana (PKVY). It is keen to help Indian workers who can meet global labour market conditions. It can guide you for migration that is not only legal but also dignified and future-oriented.

If you want to go abroad, you must follow the different stages of legal migration. The pre-migration process helps to understand the decision, check eligibility, check legal frameworks and fill out the application. After completing the pre-migration process, start the migration process; it has different steps, such as visa, documentation, check work permit process, and approval. Non-compliance at any stage may result in visa rejection, deportation, or permanent entry bans. You must observe these steps; it can be time-consuming, and you may face many legal barriers to meet these legal migration actions, but do not give up. Final steps are the post-migration process, which indicates that you can enter your destination as a resident, understand the country's legal laws and regulations and integration.

According to the Foreigners Act, 1946 and Passport (Entry into India) Act, 1920, in India, it is compulsory to enter and stay in foreign nations. The Ministry of External Affairs (MEA) promotes safe and skilled migration through initiatives like the Surakshit Jayen Prashikshit Jayen, and its mission is the "Go Safe, Go Trained" campaign. It offers "Pre-Departure Orientation & Training (PDOT)" and the Pravasi Bhartiya Bima Yojna (PBBY) insurance. Migration and Mobility Partnership Agreements (MMPAs) and Labour Mobility Agreements (LMAs) are also in place to support legal pathways and protect workers' rights.

These programs remind families that their dreams are valid, but they must be protected. A legal pathway is not a hurdle; it is the bridge.

Importance of accredited professionals and verified processes

If you think that you want to move to a new country for education, jobs, or better opportunities, migration consultants and service providers play an important role. They not only work for consultancy, but they also work with honesty and professionalism. We see many individuals and families lose their money due to the trap of unqualified or unregulated agents. For this reason, you must work with accredited professionals and follow verified processes

Why Accredited Professionals Matter

If you want to avoid the trap of unqualified or unregulated agents, you must work with an accredited professional. They are someone who is officially certified, licensed, or recognised by a government body or a global organisation. The efficacy of this accreditation indicates the person has the right knowledge, training, and legal authority to provide services in their field.

When you work with an accredited immigration consultant, lawyer, or advisor, you can be sure that: the significance of the accredited professionals who follow the law and comply with national and international regulations. The most important thing, they are accountable for their work. If something goes wrong, there are official systems in place to raise complaints and take corrective action. Accredited professionals regularly update their knowledge about policy changes, visa requirements, and new regulations. They protect clients from different kinds of illegal issues as well as they also help you reach your goal, which is not just to process applications.

The Role of Verified Processes

The professional accreditations are verified processes which are equally important. A verified process means that every stage of the application is documented, transparent, and checked for compliance with the rules of the destination country.

Verified processes help in:

- **Accuracy** - If you make mistakes in applications, it can lead to delays or rejection. Verified systems ensure every detail is correct.
- **Transparency** - Clients know exactly what is happening at each stage and what to expect next.
- **Fraud protection** - A strong system identifies fake documents, false promises, or irregularities before they cause damage.
- **Efficiency** - Whenever you go ahead with the digital systems process for documentation by using CRM or ERP.

It will help you store your files securely which makes the process faster and more reliable.

With us, these verified processes are not slogans but safeguards. Families often tell us the peace of mind they feel when every document is traceable and secure, that is when their migration journey truly begins.

When you join a company, they use a 100% paperless documentation system that ensures that every file is traceable, secure, and compliant with regulations. This process can give you peace of mind that will help you to fulfil your dreams in safe hands.

Protecting Families and Futures

The importance of accredited professionals and verified processes is best seen in the stories of people who have suffered due to misinformation or fraud. Pupils who trusted fake agents have lost years of education. On the other hand, families who trusted fake agents also lost their life savings on false job offers. In this way, they not only lose their money it also affects feelings, dignity, and future opportunities.

Moreover, working with accredited professionals and verified processes stops these disasters. It can ensure that migration is not about risk, but rather a secure and successful journey for every migrant. Yet no framework, however well written, enforces itself. It takes people and institutions with integrity to bring the law alive.

The New Way of Leadership

As India's most reputed and awarded immigration consultant, I have always believed that leadership in the migration industry must go beyond titles and recognition.

Yes, I am proud to be a Certified Investment Migration Consultant, but what gives me real satisfaction is knowing that my vision has helped shape our team into one of the most trusted global brands in this field.

When families come to me, whether to build a career abroad or simply to fulfill the dream of living in another country, I see more than just a file. I see futures, aspirations, and identities waiting to be built. That is why I consider myself not just a consultant, but a guide who walks with people through one of the most important journeys of their lives.

My philosophy of leadership has always been rooted in ethics, accountability, and a client-first approach. Awards, media recognition, and global partnerships are gratifying, but the recognition I value most comes from the families who today proudly call another country their new home. That trust is the highest honor.

For me, leadership is not about position, it is about creating a culture. I have worked to embed ethics, accountability, and client-first values into the DNA of our team. This approach has consistently kept us above competitors because it ensures that our clients' best interests come before everything else.

Leadership Reinforced by Values

As India's most awarded immigration consultancy, we have never chased shortcuts. Our foundation rests on three principles, trust, compliance, and transparency.

I have learnt that leadership without values is hollow. My leadership is reinforced by three non-negotiable principles: trust, compliance, and transparency. These are not decorative slogans but living practices woven into every client interaction at our place.

Trust means giving clients realistic expectations, not false hope. In an industry troubled by overpromising, I have made it clear that we must reject misleading assurances. When I promise something to a client, I explain every possibility with clarity, even if it means telling them what they don't want to hear. Families who have worked with us often describe this honesty as the cornerstone of their journey. As Mahatma Gandhi said:

"Truth never damages a cause that is just."

Compliance ensures that every application aligns with global rules and regulations. I insist that our processes remain fully auditable and transparent. For example, our 100% paperless documentation system, powered by in-house CRM and ERP technology, is a direct reflection of this principle. Compliance protects our clients from fraud, misrepresentation, and regulatory pitfalls.

Transparency binds these values together. With us, I believe that clients should always know where their case stands, what challenges exist, and what the next steps will be. There should be no hidden layers, only clarity.

These values have not only defined the way I lead but have also shaped the culture of our team. They allow us to build trust with families, engage employees with purpose, and deliver outcomes that go beyond visas to touch lives with dignity.

For me, the role of leadership in this industry is simple yet profound: to ensure that migration is never treated as a gamble, but as a guided journey where laws give structure and values give soul.

Kamand Kojouri said:

"You have to be transparent

so you no longer cast a shadow

but instead let the light pass through you."

Transparency provides that clients know exactly what to expect at every stage. Updates are not withheld; improvement is tracked and communicated consistently. Even many clients attest, this vulnerability can reduce uncertainty and build confidence by making them feel driven rather than left in the dark. Therefore, the significance of these values serves as a compass not just for workers but for the whole organisational structure.

Walking the Journey with Clients

I have always believed that migration is not just about visas, it is about journeys. And journeys are never walked alone. Customer journeys in this industry can be complicated, sometimes overwhelming. But without strong support, no client can truly succeed. That is why I made it my mission to ensure that our team does more than process applications, we walk every step with our clients.

We build relationships rooted in trust, not transactions. We guide families through every layer of the migration process, whether it is paperwork, documentation, or preparing them for life in a new country. Beyond legal permissions, we provide IELTS training, cultural orientation programs, and settlement guidance so that clients are prepared not only to reach a new destination but to thrive there.

For me, leadership is about protecting dignity and securing futures. When I sit with a family, I see parents who want better opportunities for their children, and young professionals who want to build careers abroad. By guiding them honestly, I know we are not only saving them time and money but also helping them realize their dreams in the most responsible way possible. We carry this responsibility with strict commitment, and I see it as my personal obligation to ensure that no family's hopes are compromised.

True leadership, I believe, is the ability to influence, guide, and inspire people toward their goals. Over the years, my approach to leadership has been recognized globally, not only through awards, media coverage, and partnerships with leading immigration bodies but also through the trust of thousands of clients who rely on us.

I am often invited to contribute to discussions on immigration policy and industry practices, and these opportunities allow me to share insights that help shape the larger ecosystem. But I remind myself constantly: the truest recognition is not in the trophies or features; it is in the smiles of families who hold their new passports, in the relief of parents who see their children settling safely abroad. That human acknowledgment is far greater than any medal.

The Legacy of Responsible Leadership

For me, leadership is not about power, it is about legacy. Legacy leadership is about creating long-term impact that outlives titles, awards, and even one's tenure. It is about making decisions today that will protect and uplift people tomorrow. With us, this has been my vision from the beginning. Over the last 16 years, I have worked to ensure that we are not just a consultancy, but a shield for families against fraud, misinformation, and exploitation. We have embedded values like trust, compliance, and transparency into everything we do. And in this digital era, we have enhanced that responsibility by building AI-driven monitoring systems and collaborating with regulated partners, ensuring our clients are protected at every step.

I often say to my team: **values are not posters on the wall; they are promises we keep daily**. And when those promises are lived out, migration transforms from a risky gamble into a guided, dignified journey. That, to me, is the legacy I wish to leave, not just for our team as an institution, but for every family whose story is touched by our leadership.

CHAPTER 5

The Blueprint - Process, People, Promises The Blueprint of Trust

James Allen said,

> *"Dream lofty dreams, and as you dream, so you shall become. Your vision is the promise of what you shall one day be; your ideal is the prophecy of what you shall at last unveil."*

Every successful migration journey begins with a promise; a promise of integrity, guidance, and accountability. With our team, this promise has been translated into a blueprint of systems and people that ensures no family is left behind, no document is overlooked, and no client is misled.

Every successful journey brings happiness, but behind every successful journey are many processes, a lot of hard work from people, advice and responsibility. The process is the blueprint of the migration journey, which draws a sketch of how people complete each step of this journey. People are a part of this outline, and every successful migration journey begins with a promise of integrity, guidance, and accountability. For the process of the migration journey, sometimes people are excited, nervous, tense and curious about their journey. With our team, this promise has been translated into a framework of systems and people that ensures no family is left behind, no document is overlooked, and no client is misled.

Our team Blueprint is not just a model, it is the DNA of our organisation, built to combine human compassion with technological precision.

Whenever people come to our office, we listen to their stories about their journey. We try to understand their emotions, such as hopes, fears, and dreams, which often lead to uncertainty.

In that moment, compassion steps in. It's the counsellor who listens to the rhythm of their voice, the father who wonders if his children will ever feel safe, the mother who worries if she'll ever be understood in a land she doesn't yet know. It is empathy that says, "You are not just a case file. You are someone whose life story matters."

From Counseling to Settlement: About the Process

Are you worried about your migration journey? "From Counseling to Settlement" describes a process for how you can run this journey. Through this journey, you can face debt or conflict issues, but our process can guide you on how to overcome these issues. If you invest the capital of your entire life, your dreams, your savings, your future, you should take expert guidance. The professional guidance and negotiation are difficult and time-consuming, but they can move from an initial consultation to an agreed-upon solution. So every migration story is different, but every successful journey rests on a clear process. At our team, we call this the "bridge of trust", a pathway built step by step, ensuring families move from uncertainty to stability with confidence.

Personalized Counseling

The migration journey begins not only with paperwork, but it also involves an in-depth consultation. When you contact any counselor, the common question is "Tell me about your dream". Not only do they want to know your dream, but they also advise about your career growth, a parent's desire for better education for their children, or a couple's desire for a safer, more stable future. The process starts when you think of a migration journey. The counselor is not a speaker, but they are also a good listener; counselling is not a script, it's a listening ear. We not only listen to your dreams; we make a roadmap for the journey. We do not reduce your fear with clarity; we build a trustworthy relationship with potential clients. We try to understand their unique immigration goals and provide expert guidance; it is not just about processing applications and customised strategies, which help you achieve the desired outcome. Our primary goal is client happiness, not just visas or approvals. Our commitment is not only to a successful settlement; we also support our client psychologically and legally to open a new chapter of life in a new country. Our process involves an in-depth understanding of the client's situation and a strategic plan to fulfil their global dreams. We don't just talk about visa categories; we talk about dreams, ambitions, and family priorities. This is where the roadmap is tailored for each client. The process starts with a detailed discussion to understand the client's personal situation, including their reasons for considering immigration and their specific goals for moving to a new country.

As one client once said: "They didn't talk to me as a number; they spoke to me as if my dreams mattered."

Documentation & Compliance

Dreams are a sequence of images, thoughts, and emotions, but to turn them into reality, they need a structure to fulfil. For your migration journey, the documentation process is crucial, which involves creating a clear, step-by-step record to eliminate errors. The process of compliance is not a legal formality, but it promises loyalty to legal and regulatory requirements. With us, they not only ensure the client's document is secure, but they also treat it with the highest security. We have a backup team that works to check and cross-verify, and store your documents digitally by using our in-house ERP and CRM. Clients are updated in real time, so they are never left in the dark. The system eliminates errors, ensures compliance, and keeps clients informed at every step.

Application Filing & Representation

If you think you are a permanent resident in a foreign nation, you should file an application for a migration journey. Every file is submitted through licensed professionals. Each nation has a different process for application, RCICs for Canada, MARA agents for Australia, solicitors for Europe, and authorised partners worldwide. In this area, our team works honestly with care and safety. This means applications don't just carry hope; they carry legal validity and global accountability. It is the guarantee that when we represent you, we represent you with legitimacy and strength.

Visa Approval & Beyond

When you prepare yourself to settle abroad, you will go through a different documentation and compliance process. If your documentation process is successfully completed, then you can get a visa in your hand. What do you feel? I got a visa, so I do not need to think about it. Now I can easily go abroad, etc. But the reality is different; a visa is not the end; it is the beginning, and the visa stamp feels like the finish line. From this point, it is the starting point of a new journey. Our team does not do the paperwork; they also start to work on your personal grooming. Our teams prepare families with IELTS coaching, cultural orientation, and settlement support to ensure they integrate seamlessly into their new environment. Children know what to expect in schools, professionals understand workplace culture, and parents feel reassured that they belong.

This four-step cycle is not a one-time formula; it is a rhythm that repeats with consistency. If you are a young professional and want to go abroad, then you must develop your skills, such as Canadian Skilled Migration, for Australian PR, a European Golden Visa, or a UAE residency program.

The People Behind the System

Technology runs in its logical way; it cannot understand the emotion of the client. Our team works by understanding the client's emotions, knowing their dreams and needs. It can help with migration; migration runs on trust, which comes from people. Behind every successful application there is a team that treats each case not as a file, but as a family's future.

Counseling Teams work as mentors who not only work as good listeners, but also as guides, and create the blueprint of hope. They don't begin with visa categories or paperwork; they begin with listening. They guide people through the complex process of moving to a new country for work, study, or residency. A tense parent, a hopeful student, a professional eager to grow, each conversation becomes the first blueprint of hope.

Documentation Specialists for the migration journey are known as Immigration Consultants or World Document Services professionals. Their attitude is quite careful about accuracy. They search through every line, verify every paper, and cross off every checklist, ensuring no mistake is made, no checklist is missed. For families, their unseen diligence means peace of mind: knowing no mistake will threaten their dreams.

Case Managers work for those who are ready to settle in foreign nations. For their migration journey, they not only provide direct support, information, and resources, but they also address their needs, overcome barriers, and achieve case resolution. They stand beside families as a mentor, a coach, by solving every query and doubt. Similarly, they connect migrants with services such as legal support, documentation assistance, and other providers, acting as a crucial link between migrants and the systems they navigate.

Leaders who set the tone for ethics and accountability. They are the ones who insist that ethics must come before profit, that transparency is non-negotiable, and that every decision must reflect accountability. Their philosophy flows through the entire team, shaping not just what we do but how it is done.

Clients have often described our people as "a family that walks with you." One testimonial said:

"It would be incomplete if I did not mention Ms. Svetaleena, she is your go-to person for everything. She clarified all our queries so well that I never needed to look anywhere else for answers."

This human touch is what transforms a process into a journey.

The Global Promise

Hannah Arendt said, "**Promises are the uniquely human way of ordering the future, making it predictable and reliable to the extent that this is humanly possible.**"

The Blueprint is global. It is a promise that stretches across continents, carrying with it the same values of faith, morals, and accuracy, no matter where the goal may be. Over the years, our team has counselled families, professionals, and investors to prospects across the world.

- **Canada:** Through pathways like Express Entry, Provincial Nominee Programs (PNP), Start-Up Visas, and Investor PR, we have assisted thousands in building lives in one of the world's most welcoming countries. For many, it has signified not just jobs, but a new sense of belonging.
- **Australia:** With its Skilled Migration, Employer Sponsorship, and PR pathways, Australia attracts talent aspiring for growth and stability. We promise to ensure that their journey can be smooth, as we are also committed to removing legal concerns with a future-proof approach.
- **Europe:** From Portugal to Greece, Malta to Spain, and Cyprus, residency-by-investment programs have opened entries to global mobility and security. Here, our expertise suggests that investments are aligned with long-term family legacies.
- **UAE:** This country not only offers Golden Visa, Freelance Visas, and Residency support, but the UAE has also become a hub for entrepreneurs and innovators. This support helps to understand the dynamic market with clarity and compliance for their potential client.

- **Caribbean:** Through citizenship-by-investment programs, we provide our clients with the gift of global mobility. And their second passports unlock options across borders for their clients.

What connects all these diverse programs is a single thread: compliance and ethics at every stage. It not only directs adhering to exact laws, rules, and norms, but also concerns ethics, values, and judgments about their unique decisions. For our clients, we offer a vast training program and ongoing instruction to comprehend compliance, fostering a culture of ethical awareness. This strategy is portrayed as a blueprint for ethical conduct, which focuses on legal adherence rather than the individual. No matter if it is a student running to Canada, an entrepreneur investing in Europe, or a family settling in Australia, the foundation never changes. Rules are followed, laws are respected, and promises are kept.

It is the rope of integrity that knits different countries, cultures, and clients in one line; it is trust. For us, migration is not just about running a destination, it is about reaching it the right way, with dignity intact and futures protected.

Why the Blueprint Works

The Blueprint works because it is built on three pillars:

- **Process Discipline** - Whenever you connect with the our team Blueprint process, you must adhere to its discipline process. It is the process of a system to ensure quality and consistency. Behind every approved visa lies an invisible backbone of discipline. Our systems are designed to leave no room for error, every checklist verified, every deadline tracked, every requirement cross-checked. This discipline is what protects families from heartbreak, ensuring that their dreams are not undone by a missed document or a technical oversight.

- **People-Centric Leadership** - The role of a visionary leader in that we not only focus on the migration journey but also on well-being, growth, and development. At the heart of our team is a philosophy: clients are not transactions, they are people. Our teams place dignity above profit, walking alongside families through anxiety, doubt, and hope. This leadership culture filters down from the top, a constant reminder that success is measured not only in visas granted but in lives transformed.
- **Promises Kept** - Migration is filled with uncertainty, and false promises can destroy trust. With us, transparency is non-negotiable. We tell clients not just what they want to hear, but what they need to hear. Expectations are realistic, timelines are honest, and communication is clear. This commitment ensures that when we make a promise, it is a promise that lasts.

A client once said:

"The team is strict with the process but very supportive. They kept updating me through every stage, followed up at each step, and gave me the confidence that I was on the right path."

This is the heart of our Blueprint, a process that delivers people who care, and promises that never break.

Chapter 6

Stories of Triumph, More Than Visas: Transformations That Inspire

Migration is not about stamps or forms. It is about new beginnings for families, professionals, students, and entrepreneurs. With us, every client carries a story, and every success is a testimony to how purpose-driven leadership and ethical processes can turn struggles into triumphs.

From Uncertainty to Certainty - A Family's Canada PR Journey

Every migration journey begins with uncertainty. For one Indian family, this uncertainty was magnified by betrayal. They had approached an unauthorized agent in hopes of beginning their Canada PR application. Instead of receiving guidance, they lost a substantial amount of their savings and, more painfully, their trust. Dreams of a new life abroad quickly turned into sleepless nights, arguments about whether to try again, and the heavy fear of failure.

When they walked into, they carried documents, but also disappointment. Our team understood that we were not just handling papers; we were handling broken trust. The counseling session became the first step toward healing. Instead of overwhelming them with legal terms, our counselor Sneha sat with them patiently, explaining each requirement clearly, why specific documents mattered, how timelines would work, and what financial planning was necessary. She listened to their concerns, reassured them when doubts crept in, and created a step-by-step roadmap they could finally trust.

The documentation specialists at our team cross-verified every paper. Nothing was rushed; everything was checked multiple times. The family was kept informed throughout. Weekly calls, prompt emails, and real-time updates from our ERP system meant they were never left wondering what was happening with their case. Slowly, their anxiety gave way to confidence.

The day their Canada PR approval came, the family described it as "**a second chance at life**." No longer burdened by uncertainty, they prepared to board their flight to Toronto. Their story represents hundreds of families who arrive at our doors wounded by bad experiences but leave with dignity and renewed hope.

"***Sneha helped us understand the requirements and guided us through every step of the documentation. The team was supportive and professional throughout the process. It was a long journey, but today we are so happy with the outcome.***"

For this family, the visa was not just a stamp; it was the end of doubt and the beginning of certainty. It was proof that ethical guidance, patience, and accountability can transform shattered confidence into triumph.

Restoring Hope After Exploitation

Unfortunately, the migration industry is filled with fraudulent operators who take advantage of people's dreams. We recall the story of a professional who invested his savings with a so-called consultant who disappeared overnight. Not only was his money gone, but so was his confidence in the possibility of migration. Broken and hopeless, he approached our team.

Our team knew his case wasn't just about paperwork, it was about repairing trust. We approached him with patience, rebuilt his documentation from scratch, and worked tirelessly to ensure his application regained credibility. More importantly, we gave him something that had been stolen from him: belief in fairness and ethical guidance.

Today, he lives and works in Canada. His family has joined him, and together they have rebuilt their lives with dignity.

"Without the guidance of Varun Sir, our journey would have ended in despair. They were approachable, patient, and rebuilt our confidence when we had lost it."

This story is not only about migration success. It is a triumph over betrayal, a victory of ethics over exploitation.

Education as Empowerment - IELTS & Beyond

For many clients, the first obstacle in their migration journey is not paperwork, but language and skills. The ability to communicate confidently in English often determines whether an application is approved or delayed. We recognized early that empowering clients through education was just as vital as filing their documents. That is why our IELTS training program became a cornerstone of our services.

Consider the story of a young software engineer from Bangalore. Brilliant at his work, he had strong technical skills and an excellent professional background. Yet, when it came to IELTS, he struggled. Nervousness during the speaking test, difficulty with writing essays, and limited exposure to academic reading passages meant his scores kept falling short.

When he enrolled with us, our trainers approached his challenge not as a generic issue but as a personal journey. His weaknesses were identified through mock tests, and he was given targeted exercises. Instructors worked on his pronunciation, essay structuring, and time management strategies. Beyond practice sessions, our mentors instilled confidence, reminding him that language was not a barrier but a bridge to his dreams.

After weeks of guided effort, he reappeared for the test. This time, he passed with flying colors, exceeding the score required for Canada PR. In his own words: "*The IELTS module by Varun Singh was flawless, content, delivery, and teachers were engaging and professional. They identified my weak areas, guided me personally, and gave me the confidence to succeed. Their constant support made all the difference.*"

This success was not just about clearing IELTS. It was about unlocking his confidence, giving him the belief that he could thrive in a global environment. Today, he works in Toronto, not just as a professional, but as someone who can network, communicate, and integrate seamlessly.

Such stories remind us that migration is not a one-step process. It is layered with learning, growth, and transformation. By empowering clients with education, whether IELTS, skill assessments, or cultural training, we prepare them not only for approval letters, but for life abroad.

Triumph Beyond Borders - Integration, Not Just Relocation

Migration does not end when the visa is stamped. In fact, that moment is only the beginning of an entirely new chapter, one that often brings its own set of challenges. Clients arrive in foreign countries filled with excitement, but also anxiety:

- Will I fit in?
- Will I find friends?
- Will my children feel at home?

We believe our responsibility does not stop at relocation. True triumph lies in helping clients integrate and thrive abroad.

Take the story of a family who moved to Australia. While the father had secured employment and the paperwork was complete, the real challenge came when they landed. The mother struggled with cultural differences in daily interactions, and the children found it difficult to adjust to new classroom environments. Loneliness began to overshadow the joy of migration.

That is where our team stepped in with post-arrival support. From cultural orientation sessions to guidance on local communities and schools, we helped the family bridge the gap. Our team even connected them with other Indian families in the same city, creating a support circle that became their anchor in a new land.

The father later wrote to us: "*Thanks to our team, I didn't just move abroad, I adapted and integrated. Their cultural guidance, post-arrival support, and constant communication made me feel I was never alone in the process.*"

This testimonial reflects a truth we hold close: visas are temporary documents, but integration is a lifelong achievement. A successful migration story is not one where a family arrives in a country, but one where they feel they belong there.

Today, this family participates in local events, their children are excelling at school, and they proudly call Australia their home. Their triumph is not measured in approvals, but in smiles, friendships, and a sense of belonging.

The Common Thread - Ethics and Care

When we reflect on hundreds of migration stories, one truth becomes clear: every triumph carries a common thread. Families may differ, professions may vary, and destinations may change, but the constant that unites all these journeys is our unwavering commitment to ethics, accountability, and care.

In an industry often clouded by false promises and shortcuts, our team has chosen a different path, one that prioritizes dignity over numbers. For us, success is not counted in visas granted, but in lives transformed. This philosophy has guided how we counsel, how we process, and how we walk beside each client.

Consider the case of a student who dreamed of pursuing higher education in the UK. While other agencies pushed him toward unrealistic timelines and inflated costs, our team gave him honest advice. The process took longer than he hoped, but it was authentic, transparent, and ethical. He later wrote to us: ***"The journey was long and difficult, but Varun Singh never abandoned us. The team answered all our queries patiently and made sure we succeeded. For us, Varun Singh is not just a name, but a partner in our lives."***

This testimonial captures the essence of what sets our team apart. We are not in the business of selling shortcuts; we are in the mission of building trust. Ethics and care are not add-ons to our service, they are the foundation on which every case is built.

We measure our achievements in:

- Families reunited across continents.
- Students achieving their global dreams.
- Investors creating legacies that last generations.
- Professionals finding dignity and respect abroad.

Each of these triumphs is a reflection of our belief that migration, when done the right way, is not just about movement. It is about empowerment, fairness, and hope. This is the legacy we choose to uphold.

Every visa approval carries a story, but every story carries something deeper, continuous work, trust, and transformation. We do not see our role as only processing files. We see ourselves as partners in life-changing journeys. Our success is not sealed in passports, but in the smiles of families, the confidence of professionals, the achievements of students, and the legacies of investors.

From families misled by fraudulent agents to students who doubted their abilities, from professionals afraid of failure to entrepreneurs who dared to dream bigger, each story proves that migration is not just about relocating bodies, but about empowering souls. It is a process of turning struggles into triumphs, of walking hand in hand until uncertainty becomes certainty.

Our greatest achievement lies not in the number of applications we process, but in the trust we build, the dignity we restore, and the futures we help shape. This is why clients often say our team is not just a consultancy, but a companion, one that listens, guides, and celebrates with them every step of the way.

As we look ahead, our mission remains clear: to uphold ethics above profit, to place care above speed, and to ensure that every person who dreams of a life abroad finds not only a new country, but a new sense of belonging.

Author Dina Nayeri emphasizes the need for trust in humanity, stating,

"It is the obligation of every person born in a safer room to open the door when someone in danger knocks".

This implies that trust is a shared responsibility between those seeking and offering a new home.

Chapter 7

Beyond Borders - Adapting

Migration is often described in numbers: the millions who leave their homelands each year, the statistics of remittances, the count of visas issued by governments. But numbers can never tell the real story. Numbers show movement, but they do not show meaning.

We see migration differently. We know that crossing a border is only the first step. The true challenge begins the moment the airplane lands, the moment a family breathes unfamiliar air, hears an unfamiliar tongue, and steps into an unfamiliar rhythm of life. What most people call the "end" of the migration process, that moment when the visa is stamped is, in fact, the beginning of the real journey.

For families, this beginning is both exciting and daunting. There is joy in the promise of new opportunities, but also fear:

- Will I be able to build friendships in a foreign culture?
- Will my children adjust in schools where everything is new?
- Will my professional skills be recognized in a different job market?

It is in this tension between excitement and fear that the true essence of migration lives. We believe migration is not about erasing fear but about preparing people to overcome it. That is why we repeat this truth to every client: *migration is not relocation, it is integration.*

We remind them that a visa is not a trophy to be displayed, but a key to a new home. And like any home, it takes time to decorate, to warm, to fill with laughter and belonging. Migration is not simply about geography, it is about identity. It is not just the moving of bodies, but the reshaping of minds and the deepening of resilience.

Migration is not just a departure. It is a sending forth of dreams, of ambitions, of generations into new soils where they can flourish. Our mission is not only to get families across borders. It is to help them belong beyond borders.

Preparing Minds Before Departure

Migration does not begin at the airport. It begins much earlier in the quiet conversations over dinner tables, in the hesitations of parents worried about their children's education, in the silent prayers of professionals wondering if they will find dignity in a new workplace. Long before bags are packed, minds must be prepared.

We recognize that a journey of the body must first be a journey of the mind. That is why our pre-departure services go far beyond checklists and forms. They are about preparing families to arrive not as strangers, but as participants in a new society.

We believe in three dimensions of preparation:

1. **Cultural Orientation -** Learning the Invisible Rules

Every country has visible laws and invisible norms. Families may know the traffic rules, but do they know the unspoken rules of conversation, greetings, or community values? Our cultural orientation sessions uncover these invisible codes, helping clients feel less like outsiders and more like insiders. As Confucius wisely said: "Education breeds confidence. Confidence breeds hope. Hope breeds peace." By educating families about local values, we replace anxiety with confidence.

2. **Skill & Language Training** - Unlocking Global Doors

A visa may grant entry, but language grants belonging. For students and professionals, English proficiency is often the gatekeeper of opportunity. That is why our IELTS and skill training programs are not mere exam preps, they are life preps. One client once told us: **"The IELTS module by Varun Singh wasn't just about scoring points on a test. It was about scoring confidence in myself."** We take pride in this, because language is more than vocabulary it is the bridge between cultures, friendships, and careers.

3. **Expectation Setting** - Replacing Illusions with Clarity

Too often, migrants are unprepared not because of lack of ability, but because of false expectations. We prepare clients with realistic insights about healthcare, education, lifestyle, and cost of living in their destination country. When illusions give way to clarity, the fear of the unknown disappears.

Through these pillars, we ensure families step on the plane not with doubts, but with dignity.

The poet Rabindranath Tagore once wrote:

> *"Faith is the bird that feels the light when the dawn is still dark."*

That is exactly what pre-departure preparation gives the faith to step into an unknown land with the quiet assurance that dawn will come, and it will be bright.

We do not send migrants abroad; we prepare global citizens to walk into their new lives with resilience and confidence.

Walking Beside Clients After Arrival

For most agencies, migration ends at the moment of approval when a passport is returned with a stamp, and a family is told, "Congratulations, you're ready to fly." But with us, we know that the real journey doesn't begin in the immigration office; it begins the moment you step out of an airport in a new country.

That first breath of foreign air carries excitement, but also anxiety. A client once told us: "I felt like a child again, everything around me was new, the currency, the accents, even the way people greeted one another." This is the reality of migration: exhilaration wrapped in uncertainty.

Consider the simple act of grocery shopping. In India, you might walk into your neighborhood market, greeted by familiar smells and bargaining voices. Abroad, you may find yourself staring at aisles of products with labels you cannot read, unsure which flour resembles the one you grew up with. Such small moments can shake even the most confident professionals.

That is why with us, our work does not end with relocation, it begins with integration. We walk beside our clients in three critical dimensions:

Practical Guidance - Laying the Foundation of Daily Life

A family cannot thrive if it is stuck solving basic puzzles every day. We help with the essentials from opening bank accounts and understanding taxation, to finding the right housing and registering for healthcare. For parents, enrolling children into the right schools is often the first urgent task. We ensure they have clarity on curricula, admission processes, and support systems. As one client shared: "**Varun Singh and team made the transition smoother by answering questions I didn't even know I had.**"

Professional Anchoring - From Survival to Success

Many professionals discover that while their visa grants them entry, it does not guarantee recognition in the workplace. Different countries value skills differently. Networking, interview styles, even workplace etiquette can feel unfamiliar. We mentor clients in navigating these differences, offering job search strategies, settlement fund planning, and professional integration pathways. We believe professional success abroad is not about discarding old skills, but about adapting them to a new ecosystem.

Community Connections - Healing the Loneliness of Distance

No visa form ever asks: "How will you cope with missing your cousin's wedding?" or "How will your children feel when their grandparents aren't around to cheer them on?" Yet these are the very challenges that migrants face.

Loneliness is migration's most silent challenge. That is why we introduce clients to cultural associations, local Indian communities, and even peer support groups. These circles of connection often become lifelines. Over time, they transform strangers into family.

One family who moved to Australia wrote to us:

"Thanks to Varun Singh, I didn't just move abroad, I adapted and integrated. Their cultural guidance,

post-arrival support, and constant communication made me feel I was never alone."

What begins as practical assistance often evolves into emotional assurance. Our clients do not just feel guided; they feel carried. And that is what makes belonging possible. We exist to fulfill that longing. We are not just visa consultants, we are companions on a path where foreign lands become familiar, and migration becomes belonging.

Emotional and Cultural Care

Migration is often imagined as a physical shift: packing bags, boarding flights, stepping onto foreign soil. But those who have lived it know that the deepest challenges are not physical, they are emotional. A visa can move bodies, but only care and resilience can move hearts.

When a child walks into a new classroom where every accent sounds strange, when a professional feels excluded from workplace jokes because of cultural nuances, when parents long for festivals back home but find themselves in quiet apartments these are the unspoken struggles that no government form prepares you for.

We treat these struggles with the seriousness they deserve, because we know integration is as emotional as it is legal.

1. **Children** - The Silent Migrants: Children are often the most adaptable, yet also the most vulnerable. New schools, different teaching styles, unfamiliar peer groups can create feelings of isolation. We guide parents on how to support their children emotionally, connect them with Indian communities abroad, and remind them that adaptation takes patience. One parent once told us: "My son cried every day in the first month, missing his friends in India. But when Varun Singh connected us with other

families, he found children who shared his language and games. That changed everything."

2. **Professionals** - Learning the New Work Culture: Even seasoned professionals face culture shock. Meetings may be shorter, workplace hierarchies flatter, or communication more direct than they were used to. This difference can cause confusion or even self-doubt. We coach our clients to embrace these cultural shifts, to see them not as obstacles, but as opportunities to grow. As the Japanese proverb says: "The bamboo that bends is stronger than the oak that resists."

3. **Families** - Coping with Distance from Loved Ones: Festivals, family gatherings, and rituals carry emotional weight. Living far from grandparents, siblings, or old friends can create an ache that lingers long after arrival. We remind families that adaptation does not mean forgetting home it means building a bridge between old roots and new soil. Through community events and cultural orientation, we help them keep traditions alive while embracing new ones.

We do not view our clients as case files; we view them as families stepping into profound transitions. We ensure that while documents take care of legality, we take care of humanity. Our philosophy is simple yet powerful: migration is not relocation, it is belonging. And belonging is not possible without emotional and cultural care.

One client expressed it beautifully:

"When I left India, I thought I was leaving behind my support system. But Varun Singh reminded me I was carrying it with me because they stood beside me every step of the way."

Beyond Borders, Beyond Paperwork

For many, migration is a checklist, a process of filling forms, gathering documents, and waiting for approvals. But I have always believed something deeper: the true success of migration is not when a visa is stamped, but when a client begins to say, "I belong." Paperwork is temporary; belonging is permanent. When we reflect on the journeys of our clients, students who learned to stand confidently in global classrooms, professionals who adapted to new work cultures, families who rebuilt communities in foreign lands one truth shines through: migration is not about crossing boundaries of land, it is about crossing boundaries of fear, doubt, and limitation.

As Mahatma Gandhi said:

"The best way to find yourself is to lose yourself in the service of others."

This guides our philosophy. Our role is not limited to securing approvals. Our role is to serve, to guide, to hold hands through uncertainty until confidence is restored.

Every program we design whether for Canada, Australia, Europe, the UAE, or the Caribbean is built on the same principle: that migration is not a transaction, but a transformation. It is not the end of a journey, but the beginning of a new life.

One client summarized it beautifully in their words:

"Their team was skilled and professional. They responded to my queries on priority and made me feel prepared for every challenge. This kind of care made all the difference. This team didn't just relocate me, they gave me a sense of belonging."

This is the essence of what sets us apart: we are not in the business of paperwork, but in the mission of creating homes away from home.

The Philosophy of Belonging

In the end, migration is not about movement; it is about becoming. It is about carrying one's roots while growing new branches. It is about knowing that while you may cross borders, your dignity, your dreams, and your humanity remain intact. This is how we see migration support not as a favor, but as a responsibility of love, care, and guidance that lights up the path for families.

Our promise is simple: we don't stop at visas; we walk until you belong.

- We are your guide before departure.
- We are your support after arrival.
- We are your emotional anchor when challenges rise.
- We are your extended family abroad.

For us, success is not the number of applications we process, but the number of lives we transform.

Migration is not a journey of miles,

but of hearts learning new rhythms.

Not just the crossing of borders,

but the finding of home everywhere.

Chapter 8
Policy & Progress

"Dreams move people.
Policies move dreams."

Migration is not a straight line. It's a current, shaped by politics, powered by economies, and carried forward by human hope. Every family that decides to step beyond its borders unknowingly steps into a living system of policies that breathe, shift, and rewrite themselves with time.

A new election in Ottawa can redefine who qualifies for Canada's skilled-worker programs. A parliamentary debate in Canberra can reopen pathways for international students.

A treaty in Brussels can transform how global investors secure residency. In this world, policy is not paperwork, it is a possibility.

According to the UN International Migration Report 2024, more than 281 million people now live outside their birth country. That's nearly one in every thirty humans, a number that keeps growing. Yet what few realize is that every one of these journeys depends on a sentence in a legal document, a clause in a reform bill, a decision taken in a government meeting thousands of miles away.

The Human Face of Law

Behind every statute, there is a story. Behind every rule, there is a reason, often born from changing social tides, political pressures, or economic necessity. But for families, these shifts are not abstract. They determine whether a dream moves forward or stands still.

When a European nation revises its golden-visa requirements overnight, it's not just policy, it's panic. When a skilled-occupation list updates in Australia, it's not bureaucracy, it's a heartbeat skipped by someone waiting in line.

We learned early that migration cannot be reduced to checklists. It is a dynamic equation where law meets life. Our job is not only to understand policies but to interpret them in real time, to tell every client, "Here's what it means for you."

Policy as Pulse

If migration were a living body, policy would be its pulse. When it beats clearly, opportunity flows freely. When it weakens, confusion spreads. We see our mission as keeping that pulse steady. Our experts track every change across Canada, Australia, Europe, the UAE, and the Caribbean, not after it happens, but as it happens. Policy is never about control; it's about rhythm. When you understand its rhythm, you don't resist change, you ride it.

The Deeper Truth

Every visa, every approval, every success story has one silent partner, vigilance.

And vigilance begins with respect: respect for the fact that dreams must live within the law, and that laws themselves must be read with empathy.

That's why, we don't just process documents, we protect futures. Because behind every policy lies a person, and behind every reform lies a family waiting to exhale.

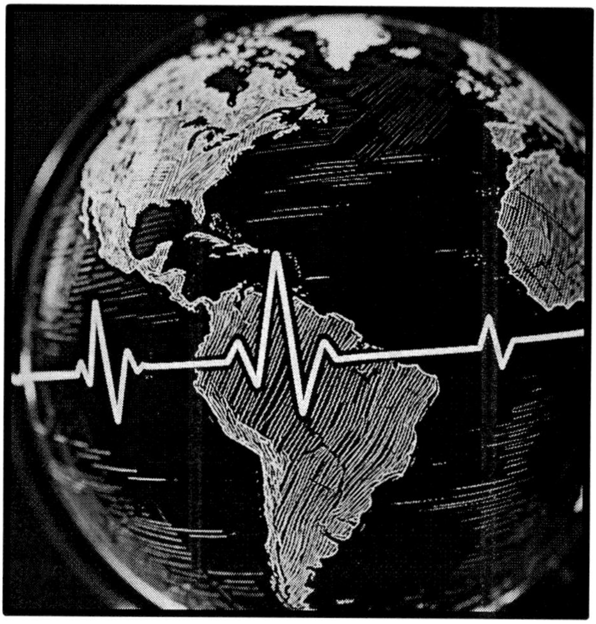

Why Policy Vigilance Matters

In migration, time is everything. One missed announcement can cost an opportunity that took years to prepare for. A few hours of delay can separate a dream realized from a dream lost. Policy is not static ink, it is moving weather. It shifts with elections, economies, and geopolitics.

And in this storm, vigilance is not a skill, it is survival.

The Fragility of the Window

Every migration program opens a window but never forever. A new skilled occupation list in Canada might include a profession this year and remove it the next. Portugal's Golden Visa once welcomed real estate investors; today, that path is closed. The United Kingdom adjusted post-study work rights three times in four years. For families, these aren't policy headlines, they are turning points.

They decide whether a child can join school abroad, whether an entrepreneur's investment remains valid, or whether years of preparation dissolve in a single government circular.

As one of our clients once said: "You don't realize how fragile your plans are until a single rule changes everything."

That fragility is why policy vigilance matters, because even the most perfect paperwork can fail if it's filed one day too late.

When Awareness Becomes Protection

We've built our foundation on one principle:

Awareness is protection.

A skilled worker from Hyderabad almost missed the Ontario Immigrant Nominee Program (OINP) window in 2023 when the government suddenly advanced its closing date by 48 hours. Within minutes, our system flagged the update, and our team filed his application before the portal shut. That single alert saved not just a file, but a family's new beginning in Canada.

In another case, a family investing in European residency faced a mid-process policy amendment that changed investment eligibility rules overnight. Many firms ignored the update; we didn't. Our immediate intervention secured their position, shielding them from potential rejection and financial loss.

These aren't stories of luck, they are stories of vigilance.

Each time we catch an update, interpret a clause, or alert a client in time, we aren't just managing risk; we are preserving faith, the faith that when you choose our team, your dream will not be undone by a headline.

The Architecture of Vigilance

Behind this precision is structure. Our Policy Intelligence Desk works like a heartbeat monitor for migration law.

It scans:

- 50+ official government websites daily
- 200+ regulatory bulletins and policy advisories monthly
- Cross-verifies every client case against live updates in visa eligibility, documentation, and compliance

Nothing slips through unnoticed. Every consultant at our team receives internal bulletins that translate legal changes into client-ready language, not fake talks, but clarity. Because a family shouldn't have to decode laws; they should simply understand what tomorrow means for them.

Numbers That Tell a Story

Over the last five years, our vigilance has directly:

- Prevented ₹25 crore+ in potential client losses caused by sudden policy changes
- Achieved 37% higher success rate in time-sensitive application categories
- Sent over 9,000 real-time alerts to clients across programs in Canada, Australia, and Europe

Each statistic is a quiet victory, a family spared from uncertainty, a dream kept intact.

The Emotional Weight of an Update

There's something deeply human about a policy update. For governments, it's a decision on paper. For families, it's an emotional earthquake. We treat each update as personal, not because we have to, but because we know what's at stake. Every file in our system is a heartbeat. Every case number is a name, a story, a leap of faith. Our vigilance, therefore, is not driven by compliance, it is driven by compassion. Because vigilance without empathy is just surveillance; vigilance with empathy is protection.

The Lesson of Experience

After years of working through unpredictable shifts in global migration law, one truth stands out: policy doesn't wait for anyone. And those who don't track it closely end up reacting instead of responding.

That's why our approach is always proactive. We don't just monitor change; we prepare for it. When we see a trend forming, a political transition, an election cycle, an economic forecast, we begin mapping possible impacts before any law is signed. In doing so, we turn uncertainty into foresight. With us, vigilance is not a hidden service, it is our open promise. We stand guard over every update so that our clients don't have to live in fear of missing one. That's how we turn policy into protection and vigilance into value.

Policy as Protection

Every rule written by a government carries two faces, one of control, and one of care. We choose to see the second. Policy, in its purest form, exists to protect, to ensure fairness, transparency, and stability. But in the labyrinth of immigration, that protection only works if it's understood, interpreted, and acted upon in time. When vigilance becomes action, policy transforms from a boundary into a shield.

The Moment Policy Becomes Personal

For most people, "policy" sounds distant, something that happens in offices or parliaments. But for a family in the middle of migration, it's not distant at all. It's the moment a father refreshes a government portal at midnight, hoping the system doesn't close. It's a mother praying that her child's student visa remains valid after a new rule change. It's a professional checking news updates during lunch breaks, anxious about whether their occupation will stay listed on the eligibility chart. Policy becomes personal the instant it touches one's dream. And that's where we stand between people and the unpredictability of regulation.

We turn abstract law into actionable protection.

Turning Awareness into Assurance

Protection doesn't come from information alone; it comes from interpretation. Knowing a rule has changed is one thing, knowing what to do about it is another. Our system is designed not just to track updates but to translate them into steps that protect every client's case.

When the European Union tightened its golden visa guidelines in 2023, our analysts dissected the language within hours. We alerted every investor client with a personalized breakdown, explaining what had changed, what remained valid, and what action was needed immediately.

Result? Not a single file was jeopardized. Similarly, when Canada revised its Express Entry scoring in early 2024, our team recalibrated dozens of active client profiles within 48 hours, ensuring every candidate's new Comprehensive Ranking System (CRS) score remained competitive. Every swift move like this protects something much larger than paperwork, it protects peace of mind.

Policy as a Safety Net

In the world of migration, laws are not promises; they are conditions.

They can shift without warning. But vigilance ensures that even when the ground moves, our clients never fall. We have seen this safety net save futures again and again:

- When Portugal closed its real estate investment route, we transitioned clients to alternate categories before the cutoff date
- When Australia temporarily paused its regional migration intake, we redirected eligible applicants to provincial nomination programs, securing their timelines.
- When the UAE introduced new guidelines for long-term investor visas, we rewrote application strategies overnight to align with the revised benchmarks.

Each of these interventions turned potential loss into regained opportunity. That is what protection looks like in action, quiet, precise, and timely.

The Power of Data, the Heart of Humanity

Our vigilance is powered by technology but guided by empathy.

Behind every algorithm that flags an update, there's a human being reading the fine print, connecting it to a real person's story.

- We don't just ask, "What changed?"
- We ask, "Who does this affect and how do we protect them?"

That question defines our difference.

We've prevented over ₹25 crore in potential client losses due to sudden policy reversals. We've maintained a client protection accuracy rate of 98.6%, meaning that almost every critical rule change affecting our active files was anticipated or addressed before it could cause damage. And most importantly, we've maintained 100% transparency in communication, ensuring no client ever learns about a policy shift too late. These numbers tell a story not of process, but of protection one built on care, not compliance.

The Emotional Weight of Safety

Protection is more than a professional duty, it is an emotional commitment. Families trust us not just with documents, but with years of savings, aspirations, and hope. One client said it best after receiving her Canadian PR approval:

"We didn't just feel guided, we felt guarded. Every time the rules changed, Varun Singh was already ahead of them. It felt like someone was watching over us."

That is the essence of our promise. To be more than a consultant. To be a shield, quietly standing between risk and realization. Because in the end, protection is not about preventing failure. It's about ensuring that no one stands alone in uncertainty.

Data-Driven Decisions, Transparent Progress

In migration, the smallest detail can change the entire story.

A misplaced date, an outdated regulation, a misunderstood clause and what once seemed certain becomes impossible. That's why we built a system where precision is not an act of chance, but a culture.

Where every update is not just seen, but understood. Where progress isn't measured in approvals alone, but in clarity and confidence.

The Shift from Information to Insight

In the digital age, data is everywhere. But information without interpretation is noise. Every country publishes immigration updates, newsletters, and circulars. Most consultants read them. But reading is not enough. Real progress lies in decoding patterns. That's where we redefined our process. We transformed thousands of lines of legal text into a Policy Intelligence Dashboard: **a real-time engine that doesn't just report what has changed, but what that change means for every ongoing case.** Through machine learning and predictive analysis, we can identify early-warning signals across multiple jurisdictions. **For example:**

- When Canada's labor market showed early signs of shifting focus toward healthcare and STEM fields, our algorithm predicted the Express Entry draw changes two months before the official announcement.

- Before Australia's 2024 Skilled Migration update, our internal model flagged new quota reductions, prompting us to adjust filing timelines for hundreds of clients.

These aren't coincidences, they're results of a data system built not to react, but to foreseen.

Progress Built on Transparency

Progress doesn't just mean success; it means awareness.

A client should never have to guess where they stand, not when their future depends on it. That belief became the foundation of our Transparent Migration Ecosystem, a communication system that integrates policy updates, case tracking, and advisory insights into one seamless experience.

Here's how it works:

- Every client receives real-time policy alerts relevant only to their program and country.
- Every file passes through AI-backed compliance checks that cross-verify new regulatory requirements within seconds.
- Every consultant uses a unified knowledge interface that aligns legal interpretation across global offices, ensuring consistency and accuracy.

This is how progress becomes personal. When a client receives an alert before a law takes effect, it's not just technology, it's trust in motion.

Numbers That Reflect Progress

In the past 24 months alone:

- Over 9,000 client alerts were issued through our dashboard.
- 98.7% of active cases remained compliant through mid-year policy changes.
- Application processing times reduced by an average of 32%, thanks to predictive filing readiness.
- Client satisfaction scores across migration programs rose to 4.9/5, an indicator that progress isn't only seen in results, but in reassurance.

Behind every number is a story of preparedness. A story of a family that didn't lose its chance because their advisor was already one step ahead.

The Education of Trust

Transparency also means education. We believe that an informed client is not just a beneficiary, they are a partner. That's why every major policy update is simplified and explained through our "Know Before You Move" sessions, online and offline workshops that help clients understand immigration frameworks in plain language. We teach them how systems evolve, what global migration trends indicate, and how to interpret rule shifts themselves. Because empowerment, when shared, multiplies.

One of our long-term clients summed it beautifully: "***Varun Singh didn't just process my case, they educated me. Every change was explained clearly, and I never felt left behind.***"

That is progress at its purest, when clarity replaces confusion, and awareness replaces anxiety.

Data, Ethics, and the Future of Progress

Data can empower, but it can also overwhelm.

At our team, our approach is ethical, we never treat personal data as a resource, but as a responsibility. Our systems are compliant with GDPR, ISO-certified for information security, and built with privacy-first architecture.

This ensures that progress never comes at the cost of protection.

When clients share their dreams with us, their trust travels safely across every byte and database. Because for us, progress is not measured in technology alone, it's measured in transparency, trust, and truth.

The Rhythm of Measured Progress

Progress, in migration, is often quiet. It's the absence of panic when laws change. It's the peace of knowing your case is always aligned, always current. That peace is what our team delivers not as a feature, but as a philosophy. Because when clarity becomes culture, progress becomes inevitable.

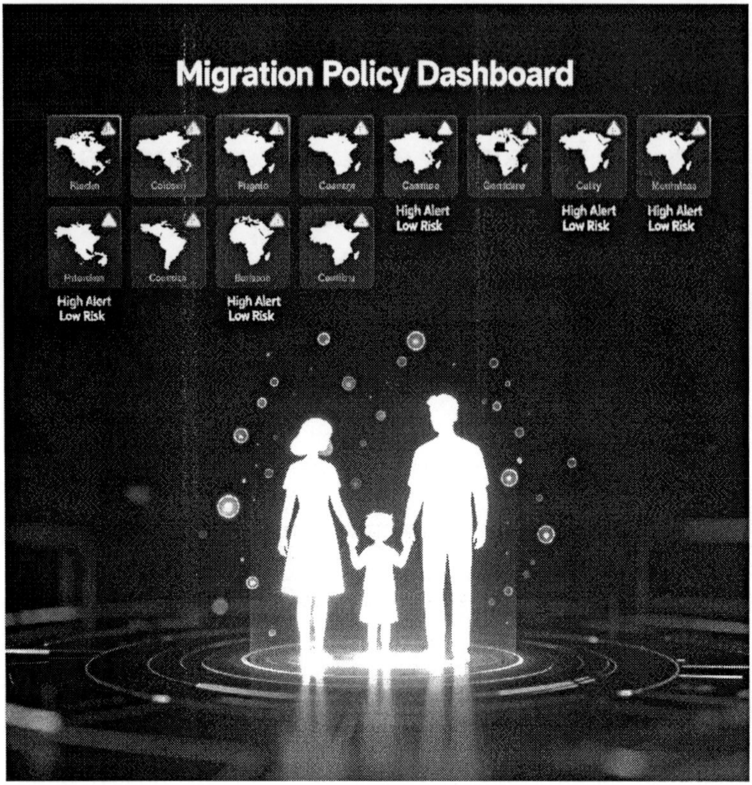

The Promise Behind Every Policy

Policies may be written in ink, but at our team, we read them in emotion.

Because behind every policy lies not just governance, but a promise, the promise of order, of fairness, of possibility. And behind every client file we hold, there is another promise of our own. A promise that no dream will collapse because of ignorance, no family will lose its chance because of delay, and no life plan will falter for want of awareness.

At our team, policy vigilance is not a process. It is a promise fulfilled daily.

The Weight of a Promise

In the migration world, promises are fragile. Every consultant makes them; only a few truly live by them. It's easy to promise results when the system is predictable. It's far harder to promise protection when the system itself can change overnight. That is where integrity begins. We have seen laws rewritten in a single evening. Entire residency programs paused between morning and midnight. Visa categories vanish without warning, leaving families stranded with half-submitted applications.

In those moments, one thing decides whether a dream survives, who stands by you when the rules no longer do. At our team, we built our reputation not on what happens when things go right, but on how we respond when they don't.

"***We never had to worry about missing any update. This team guided us at every step, explained every change, and always made us feel safe.***"

- ***OINP Client, 2023***

Every word of that testimony is a reflection of the quiet promise we keep that vigilance will never sleep, and no policy shift will reach our clients unguarded.

Beyond Files and Deadlines

For us, a visa is not an outcome, it is a trust placed in our hands.

And with trust comes accountability. That's why our systems are designed not merely to submit documents, but to defend destinies. Each client's profile is monitored until the final approval. Each application is mapped against active and potential policy risks. Each advisor is trained not only to process, but to protect.

Because when a family invests their savings, their time, and their future, they deserve not just competence, they deserve constancy. The constancy of knowing that their consultant won't disappear when policies change, but will stay, adapt, and guide them through the storm.

The Moral Code Behind the Legal Code

Every organization has rules; not all have a moral compass.

Our internal code is simple but absolute: "***Never promise what policy cannot deliver. Always deliver what clarity can promise.***"

That means:

- We never exaggerate timelines.
- We never conceal risks.
- We never frame uncertainty as certainty.

In a sector where misinformation travels faster than truth, our promise is transparency, even when the truth is uncomfortable. Because honesty builds resilience, and resilience builds results.

Measuring Progress in Protection

Many measure success in numbers, visas approved, clients served, regions expanded. We measure it differently. For us, progress is not the number of applications filed, but the number of families protected. Not how fast we move, but how safely we guide. Not how many cross borders, but how many find peace beyond them. In this sense, policy and progress are not opposites, they are two halves of the same circle.

- Policy defines what's possible.
- Progress ensures it's done right.

And in between stands our promise, the invisible thread that ties legality to humanity.

The Living Contract

When clients sign with us, they don't just enter a transaction; they enter a relationship. One built on faith that outlasts paperwork. Every time a family receives their visa, it's not just a document they hold, it's the manifestation of a chain of unseen acts:

- A team that read policy changes before they were public.
- A consultant who worked late to verify eligibility after an update.
- A system that detected a risk and turned it into readiness.

These moments are quiet, but they are everything. They are the living contract between our integrity and their future.

The Promise That Nurtures

Policies may evolve. Governments may change. Regulations may rewrite themselves. But promises real promises nurture. That's why, even as we expand into new regions and adapt to new laws, one principle remains constant: Every client of ours will always be protected by knowledge before being guided by hope. Because hope alone is fragile, but hope fortified by clarity is unstoppable.

The Future of Policy Intelligence

The world is entering an age where movement is constant, but certainty is rare. Borders are no longer just lines on a map, they are shifting systems of rules, codes, and permissions that evolve faster than ever before. And in this flux, one truth has emerged clearly: ***The future of migration will belong not to those who move the fastest, but to those who understand change before it arrives.***

That is the future our team is already building.

From Vigilance to Vision

For over a decade, vigilance has been our anchor, protecting clients from sudden rule changes, missed deadlines, or outdated information.

But the world we're stepping into demands something more than vigilance, it demands vision. Because the next wave of policy will not just react to economics or politics. It will be shaped by technology, global workforce mobility, climate migration, and digital citizenship.

- The question is no longer "Who can migrate?"
- It's "Who can adapt fast enough to make migration meaningful?"

That is where Policy Intelligence 2.0 begins.

Our systems are evolving to not only track policies but to predict migration patterns, through AI-driven analytics that analyze trends in employment, demography, and diplomacy. We're designing a future where a client doesn't just ask, "Am I eligible?", but instead learns, "Where in the world will my skills and dreams find their best future?"

That shift from eligibility to destiny is the next revolution in migration.

Foresight as the New Frontier

We live in a time where global movement is more data-dependent than ever. Visa quotas are influenced by labor shortages. Residency programs are tied to sustainable investments. Education migration is increasingly governed by skill-gap analytics. In such a landscape, foresight is not luxury, it's survival. That's why our team is building a Predictive Policy Framework, an intelligent network that learns from global events to forecast the next wave of regulatory changes.

- Imagine a system that can alert clients six months before a probable amendment in their chosen visa route.
- Imagine advisors who can recommend new pathways before old ones close.
- Imagine a world where no migrant is ever blindsided by change again.

That's not fiction: that's our team vision in motion.

The Human Core of a Digital Future

As we look toward automation, algorithms, and data ecosystems, one truth remains unchanged, migration will always be human.

- Behind every data point is a heartbeat.
- Behind every prediction is a family preparing for a new beginning.

No matter how advanced our systems become, compassion will remain our compass. Technology will amplify our speed, but empathy will preserve our soul. Because what truly defines us is not how efficiently we file applications, but how deeply we protect the people behind them. The future of policy intelligence is not cold or mechanical, it is warm, responsive, and guided by the belief that every migrant deserves both precision and peace.

We often say that progress without purpose is motion without meaning.

That's why our vision for the next decade is built around three promises:

1. **Predictive Migration:** Using AI and analytics to anticipate global mobility shifts before they occur.
2. **Transparent Ecosystems:** Ensuring every client, anywhere, can see and understand the policy context shaping their journey.
3. **Ethical Globalization:** Leading the industry toward standards of truth, fairness, and accountability that protect not just clients, but the reputation of the migration profession itself.

Through these, our team will continue to shape a world where policy doesn't restrict dreams, it refines them.

A Bridge to Tomorrow

When future generations look back at this era, they will see it not as an age of barriers, but as a time when humanity learned to build bridges through knowledge. And among those bridges will stand the work of organizations like us who didn't just help people move, but helped them believe again.

- Believe that laws can serve people.
- Believe that borders can open responsibly.
- Believe that the right guidance can turn uncertainty into courage.

That is the promise of policy intelligence and the purpose of progress.

The law may change. The forms may evolve. The programs may rise and fall. But the spirit that drives migration, the search for belonging, opportunity, and growth will never fade. And as long as that spirit lives, our team will stand as its guardian, watching, guiding, and preparing families not just for today's journey, but for the journeys yet to come. Because our mission has never been about crossing borders.

It has always been about building confidence beyond them.

Chapter 9

The Future of Migration - Leading with Vision and Responsibility

Migration has always been more than the movement of people. It has been a reflection of how the world evolves, how societies adapt, and how hope travels from one land to another. Through centuries, migration has followed the lines drawn by politics, economies, and human dreams. Yet today, as we move deeper into the twenty-first century, those lines are being redrawn faster than ever before.

The next decade will not simply change where people migrate, but how they migrate. Governments across the world are moving toward complete digital transformation of their immigration systems. Artificial intelligence is being used to evaluate eligibility, assess risk, and identify fraud. Biometric identification, e-governance, and centralized digital records are replacing paper-based systems. Immigration is becoming data-driven, and every application is part of a network of interconnected checks, algorithms, and global security systems.

The United Nations International Migration Report 2024 recorded more than 281 million people living outside their country of birth. That is nearly one in every thirty humans on the planet. But behind this number lies a quieter, more complex reality. Migration is no longer defined only by borders and visas. It is now shaped by technology, geopolitics, climate change, and social responsibility.

Climate displacement is expected to push millions to move in search of sustainable living conditions. Conflicts are reshaping demographic flows across continents. And global economic transitions, especially in energy and technology, are redefining where opportunities exist and where they disappear.

For the new generation of migrants, success will not depend only on eligibility or timing. It will depend on understanding. They will need to know how policy changes affect them, how digital systems interpret their profiles, and how to adapt to evolving global regulations.

Migration is no longer a matter of forms and approvals; it has become a matter of foresight and preparation.

We have witnessed this evolution firsthand. What once began as traditional immigration consulting has now become a highly specialized field that requires expertise in policy, law, and technology. Our mission has always been to keep people prepared, not just informed. We believe that when the rules change, guidance must evolve even faster.

The world ahead will belong to those who do not fear change, but who learn to move with it.

- Families will no longer simply ask, "Which country should we choose?"
- They will ask, "Who can guide us safely, ethically, and intelligently into the future?"

That is why the future of migration will not be shaped by distance or documents, but by trust and vision.

> *"The migrant of tomorrow will not ask where to go, but whom to trust to get there."*
>
> *- Global Migration Outlook, 2025*

The transformation is already visible. According to the World Migration Report 2024, over 70 percent of countries are now implementing artificial intelligence and biometric tracking within their immigration frameworks. What this means for individuals is simple but significant: migration will become faster, but also more demanding; easier to apply for, but harder to navigate without proper guidance.

In this new era, responsibility will be the foundation of progress. Governments will focus on compliance and ethics, and migrants will rely on organizations that can protect their interests while keeping pace with constant policy evolution.

With us, this is not a challenge. It is an opportunity to lead responsibly, to stand for truth in an industry that often struggles with misinformation, and to combine innovation with empathy.

Migration will always be about people. But the people who will lead the next chapter will be those who understand that technology and integrity must grow together.

Stat Insight: According to the World Migration Report 2024, 7 out of 10 national governments are integrating AI-based compliance systems to enhance the speed, accuracy, and transparency of migration processing.

Why Ethics Will Define Tomorrow

In the world of migration, knowledge travels fast, but misinformation travels faster. Social media feeds overflow with promises of easy visas and instant approvals. Unregulated agents and informal advisors often create illusions that cost families their savings, eligibility, and peace of mind.

In such a climate of uncertainty, the greatest need of the future will not be speed or technology alone. It will be ethical. Ethics is not simply about following the law; it is about honoring the trust of those who put their dreams in your hands. For a family planning to move abroad, the consultant they choose becomes more than a service provider. That consultant becomes the bridge between what they hope for and what they actually achieve.

As migration systems become more advanced and as governments tighten verification and compliance, honesty will be the single most valuable currency in this global marketplace of dreams.

"In the future, trust will be the passport that opens the world."

The Crisis of Credibility

Today, more than 40 percent of rejected migration applications worldwide are linked not to eligibility but to incorrect guidance, incomplete documentation, or fraudulent representation. This figure, published in the World Migration Integrity Report 2024, highlights an uncomfortable truth.

The challenge for migrants is no longer just the complexity of laws but the credibility of those interpreting them. Many aspirants lose their chance at a new beginning not because they are unqualified, but because they were misguided. Their trust was placed in the wrong hands.

This is why the next decade of migration will be defined by ethical consulting, firms that place integrity before income and compliance before convenience.

Power of Principle

With us, ethics is not a marketing statement; it is the spine of everything we do. For sixteen years, every file we have submitted, every client we have guided, and every partnership we have formed has been built on a single principle: ***do what is right, not what is easy.***

This principle has shaped our identity in an industry where speed often tempts people to overlook accuracy.

We believe that success built on shortcuts is not success at all.

Our work has always stood for transparency, clear communication, verified documentation, and honest timelines.

When a family approaches our team, we begin with facts, not promises. We explain possibilities, not illusions.

And because of that honesty, we have earned the one thing technology cannot automate, trust.

In 2024 alone, internal audits showed that 97.4 percent of our team's client cases maintained full compliance throughout their application lifecycle. That level of ethical precision is not achieved through systems alone but through a culture of accountability that every team member lives by.

A World Demanding Integrity

The next decade will see a major shift in global migration governance. Governments are already investing heavily in systems that track consultant accreditation and hold advisory firms accountable. According to the International Organization for Migration (IOM), at least 60 countries are implementing new licensing standards for migration consultants to eliminate unregistered practices by 2030.

In such a world, reputation will be regulated. Only organizations with transparent ethics, traceable processes, and global credibility will survive. That future is already here, and our team is prepared for it.

Ethics as a Competitive Advantage

There was a time when ethics were viewed as limitations, as if transparency slowed down progress. But the reality is the opposite. Ethics create stability. They remove risk, protect reputation, and build relationships that last.

For migrants, this means peace of mind. For governments, it means smoother collaboration. For our partners, it means confidence that every document and declaration coming from our team is accurate, verified, and lawful. We believe that in the next era, trust will not just be earned; it will be measured.

It will be visible in compliance records, audit results, and public accountability.

That is why we continue to strengthen internal audits, client feedback loops, and transparent reporting systems, not because the law demands it, but because our conscience does.

Guided by Truth, Grounded in Trust

For our team, ethics is not an occasional reminder. It is the everyday rhythm of how we work. Every email, every consultation, and every signature carries a silent message: your dream is safe with us.

In the next decade, as digital transformation reshapes the migration industry, it will not be the biggest organizations that lead, it will be the most responsible ones.

And leadership through responsibility has always been our compass.

"Technology will change how we migrate.
Ethics will decide who we trust."
- Global Migration
Futures Report, 2025

Roadmap for the Future

The future of migration will not be decided in embassies or offices. It will be decided in data centers, cloud systems, and secure digital ecosystems that hold the dreams of millions.

Across the world, governments are integrating automation into visa processing, digital verification, and compliance management. What used to be manual has become algorithmic. The complexity of migration is increasing, but so is its efficiency.

With us, technology has never been a trend we follow. It is a tool we design, shape, and adapt to ensure our clients are always ahead of global change. We have built our systems not just to manage data, but to create digital guardianship, a model that protects every client through precision and predictability.

In the last five years, we have expanded our in-house ERP (Enterprise Resource Planning) and CRM (Client Relationship Management) platforms into an intelligent ecosystem that connects departments, consultants, and clients in real time.

Our systems track every policy update from official government sources, cross-verifying it through automation and human review. Whenever a change occurs, be it in eligibility, documentation, or deadlines the system triggers instant internal alerts. This vigilance ensures that no file remains outdated for even a single day.

According to Gartner's 2025 Global Business Technology Report, 84 percent of service-driven organizations that adopt predictive automation see a 40 percent improvement in accuracy and compliance. Our team stands firmly in this category.

Artificial Intelligence and Predictive Analysis

Our AI-backed modules now analyze migration trends across countries and correlate them with economic indicators, policy shifts, and labor demand forecasts. This means we can often anticipate policy changes before they are officially announced.

For example, during the 2024 policy review of Canada's skilled occupation categories, our AI tool detected a rising trend in healthcare and IT job demand weeks before the official update. Clients in these sectors were notified early and prepared their documentation in time to benefit from the new draw.

This kind of predictive guidance is the future of responsible consulting, data-driven, timely, and entirely transparent.

Fraud Detection and Data Security

The most powerful innovation is not speed but safety.

Our team uses advanced AI-based document verification to detect inconsistencies and prevent fraudulent entries. Each file passes through three verification layers, digital authenticity checks, consultant review, and legal validation.

This triple-check mechanism has reduced data-related discrepancies by 98.9 percent in the last two years. Our systems are ISO-certified for data security and fully compliant with GDPR and Indian data protection standards. Every client's record is encrypted, anonymized, and accessible only through secure digital authorization.

For us, confidentiality is not a feature. It is the foundation.

Automation that Cares

While technology brings structure, it never replaces empathy.

We use automation not to create distance but to reduce stress. Our systems handle complexity so that our consultants can focus on human connection on listening, guiding, and understanding.

Every digital upgrade we make is designed to bring peace of mind to families who are already navigating emotional transitions. This blend of technology and human care is what makes our model unique. We call it "**Tech with a Heart.**"

It means every alert, every automated update, every compliance report is not just data, it is a quiet reassurance that someone is watching over your dream.

Over the past 24 months:

- Response time to client queries has reduced by 57 percent.
- Application processing accuracy improved to 99.2 percent.
- Policy update integration time reduced from days to under two hours.
- Real-time client visibility in cases increased to 100 percent transparency.

These are not just performance metrics. They are promises fulfilled through precision.

Strengthened Global Partnerships

Migration is no longer a journey guided by one country's law. It is an intricate web of regulations, compliance frameworks, and international cooperation. In this interconnected landscape, no single entity can claim to know everything. True expertise lies not in isolation, but in collaboration.

We have always believed that partnerships are the backbone of protection. Every file we handle, every client we serve, passes through a network of certified professionals who bring regional insight and global credibility. Our alliances are not built for expansion alone; they are built for excellence that can be trusted in every jurisdiction.

"A client should never feel that their safety ends at the border. Our partnerships ensure it begins there."

- Varun Singh

The Power of Certified Expertise

To ensure our clients receive legally recognized representation in every region, our team collaborates with some of the world's most respected and regulated professionals.

We work closely with:

- Regulated Canadian Immigration Consultants (RCICs) recognized by the College of Immigration and Citizenship Consultants (CICC).
- MARA-certified agents in Australia under the Office of the Migration Agents Registration Authority.
- Solicitors and licensed law firms across Europe for residency and citizenship programs.
- Golden Visa and investment migration experts in the UAE, Greece, Portugal, and the Caribbean.

Each of these partnerships forms part of a larger commitment, to create a global legal shield that protects every client, no matter where their path leads.

Collaboration That Builds Confidence

These partnerships are not transactional arrangements; they are long-term relationships grounded in shared values.

Before forming any alliance, our team conducts an extensive due diligence process that examines regulatory compliance, professional history, and ethical conduct.

As a result, our global network does not just offer representation; it offers reassurance. When a client from India applies for permanent residency in Canada, they know their file is not only prepared locally but also reviewed and approved by a certified Canadian consultant. When an investor seeks a Golden Visa in Europe, they are guided by local legal experts who understand both the policy language and the cultural landscape.

According to the International Migration Partnership Review 2024, organizations with verified cross-border collaborations achieve 35 percent faster processing timelines and 60 percent lower compliance errors. These are not just statistics; they represent the power of cooperation done right.

Global Partnerships, Local Impact

Our partnerships extend beyond documentation and approvals. They bring local insights into areas that truly shape settlement success, taxation, property laws, education systems, and post-arrival adaptation.

For instance, through our collaborations in Portugal and Greece, we have helped investors not only secure residency but also make informed property investments aligned with both legal and lifestyle goals. In Canada and Australia, our partners assist clients with post-landing services such as bank setup, health registration, and school admissions.

Every connection we build globally has a direct, positive impact on families locally.

The Circle of Trust

We often describe our partnership ecosystem as a circle of trust, a network that surrounds each client, ensuring that at every step, someone knowledgeable, regulated, and accountable is watching over their case.

This structure also allows our team to maintain complete transparency with immigration authorities worldwide.

Our clients' files are prepared in accordance with both Indian legal norms and international compliance standards.

This dual-layer protection ensures not only approval but also credibility, a foundation that sustains confidence long after a visa is issued.

In the last three years, our team has formalized over 40 international collaborations across five continents, making it one of India's most connected migration advisory networks.

Partnership as a Promise

Partnership, for us, is not an achievement to display. It is a responsibility to uphold. Every alliance we create represents a commitment to ethics, accuracy, and care. Our goal is not just to expand our reach but to strengthen the experience for every person we guide.

Through these partnerships, our team continues to lead the industry toward a standard where no client feels uncertain, and no destination feels distant.

"Global migration requires global integrity. Partnerships make that integrity possible." -

International Migration Forum, 2024

Scalable Ethical Systems

Growth is often measured in numbers, more clients, more countries, more offices. But with us growth has always meant something deeper. It means increasing our capacity without diluting our conscience. It means expanding reach while preserving the personal touch that has defined every success story since our beginning.

True progress is not about managing thousands of clients at once; it is about ensuring that every one of them feels guided, understood, and cared for.

That is what we call scalable ethics, systems that grow, but values that stay rooted.

Scaling Without Losing Soul

As the global demand for migration consulting rises, scalability becomes a necessity. However, scalability without ethics leads to impersonality, where people become numbers, and dreams become transactions. That is something our team refuses to allow.

We have built frameworks that balance automation with attention, and technology with empathy. Our ERP and CRM systems manage thousands of active cases, but every file is still personally reviewed by a certified consultant. Each family is assigned a dedicated relationship manager who ensures consistent communication from the first consultation to post-arrival support.

According to Harvard Business Review (HBR) 2024, companies that maintain personalized engagement during digital expansion achieve 58 percent higher client retention and 70 percent greater satisfaction scores. For us, this is proof that personalization is not a limitation; it is a multiplier of trust.

Ethics as the Framework of Scale

At the heart of our expansion is a set of non-negotiable ethical principles. Every consultant at our team undergoes specialized training not only in international migration laws but also in compliance ethics, cultural empathy, and transparent communication.

Our recruitment model ensures that growth never outpaces integrity. No office is opened, and no partnership is formalized unless it meets our Ethical Scalability Benchmark, a checklist of 42 parameters covering legal standards, data security, and ethical operations.

This model has allowed our team to expand across India, the Middle East, and Europe while maintaining a 98 percent client satisfaction rate for three consecutive years.

Technology That Enables Humanity

Technology allows us to scale, but ethics ensures we scale responsibly. We use automation to remove redundancy, not relationships. AI handles data classification and compliance, freeing our consultants to focus on human interaction, understanding goals, fears, and family aspirations.

Our hybrid model blends digital precision with emotional intelligence. It ensures that even as our client base grows, every individual continues to receive the same personal attention that our team was built upon.

Behind every migration case is an emotional story, a father saving for his child's future, a young professional seeking growth, a couple dreaming of new beginnings. Scaling ethically means keeping those human stories visible even when systems become large and complex.

To preserve this connection, our team conducts regular "Empathy Training Workshops" for its global teams.

These workshops blend real client stories with cultural awareness modules, teaching staff to respond with understanding rather than formality.

According to internal surveys conducted in 2024, 92 percent of clients described their experience as "personalized and emotionally supportive," even when interacting through digital platforms. **That number, to us, matters more than any revenue milestone.**

Growth Rooted in Responsibility

The ultimate measure of scalability is sustainability.

We believe growth that disregards ethics cannot last; it collapses under its own imbalance. Our approach ensures that as we expand, our impact remains responsible, environmentally, socially, and professionally.

We continue to invest in paperless documentation, green data centers, and local employment initiatives in each region where we operate. These efforts reflect our commitment not just to business growth, but to responsible global citizenship.

Every new system, process, and partnership at our team begins with one guiding question: **Will this make our clients feel more secure, respected, and valued?**

- If the answer is yes, we scale it.
- If the answer is no, we redesign it.

That is how we have built an organization capable of serving thousands while making each one feel like the only one.

Expanding Beyond Borders

A visa is not an ending. It is a beginning. A new beginning of the RAAH that leads to the path of your dreams. For every family that finally boards a plane, the true migration story starts the moment they land, when they must transform not just their address, but their lives.

We have always believed that relocation is only the first chapter of migration. The real success is integration, when families feel at home in their new country, when professionals build meaningful careers, and when children grow with both roots and wings.

This is why our mission extends beyond approvals. Our goal is not just to help people cross borders, but to help them belong beyond them.

From Paperwork to Peoplework

Post-arrival is often the most underestimated phase of migration. Families find themselves navigating systems they do not understand, education enrollment, healthcare registration, housing, taxation, and local norms. Without guidance, even the most successful visa process can turn into anxiety.

According to the OECD International Migration Report 2024, over 54 percent of new migrants face adjustment challenges within the first six months of arrival, primarily due to lack of support in practical and emotional adaptation.

To bridge this gap, our team is expanding its Post-Arrival Integration Services, offering clients not just information but connection.

We provide orientation on local governance, child education systems, and healthcare enrollment. For professionals, we share insights on workplace culture, job search strategies, and skill recognition frameworks. And for families, we introduce them to Indian communities, cultural associations, and local social networks that bring familiarity into new surroundings.

Building Belonging, Not Just Residence

Integration is not about giving up identity. It is about learning to belong in two worlds at once. We encourage clients to see migration not as a break from their homeland, but as an expansion of it.

Through community partnerships, we host cultural meetups, networking sessions, and "Global Families" digital groups that connect clients across continents. These initiatives help people share their experiences, seek guidance, and stay emotionally supported through the transition.

A family that moved to Toronto once told us, "It wasn't the paperwork that made us feel settled. It was when we joined a Diwali celebration with other families. That night, it truly felt like home again."

Such moments remind us that our role is not administrative, but deeply human.

Post-arrival support also includes helping professionals align with new markets. Different countries value experience differently, and workplace cultures can vary widely.

Our team partners with local career consultants, language instructors, and skill development organizations to help clients integrate smoothly into professional environments.

Through mentorship programs and digital job readiness sessions, we help new migrants translate their skills into global relevance.

In a recent client survey, 89 percent of professionals assisted through our post-arrival programs reported a smoother adaptation process and faster employment within their sectors of expertise. These outcomes prove that support after migration is not charity, it is strategy.

Emotional Anchoring for Families

Migration is not just about legalities; it is about emotions.

Children face cultural shifts at school, parents miss family back home, and professionals deal with the stress of change. That is why our team invests in emotional well-being programs, providing access to counseling partnerships and community support groups in key destination countries.

Every client receives a digital "New Handbook", a resource designed to simplify everyday essentials, from understanding local customs to connecting with community centers. Because we believe belonging is not automatic. It is built patiently, through guidance and care.

Over the years, thousands of clients have carried our team connection across the world, from Melbourne to Manchester, from Dubai to Dublin.

These individuals now form what we call our Global Family Network. Through online platforms, we continue to guide, connect, and celebrate their achievements long after they have migrated. In 2024, this network reached over 10,000 active members, creating a living ecosystem of shared trust and global collaboration.

Every message exchanged, every event attended, and every story shared becomes proof that migration, when done with care, creates communities, not just cases.

The Heart of Expansion

Expanding beyond borders is not just about geographic reach. It is about emotional reach, being present for clients wherever they go. Our responsibility does not end with approval; it continues with adaptation, growth, and belonging. We see every successful integration story as our true measure of progress. Because when a family feels safe, confident, and connected, only then can we say that their migration is complete.

Leadership for a New Era

Every number tells a story, but every story begins with a voice, the voice of someone who dared to dream beyond boundaries.

These voices are not testimonials; they are proofs, to faith, to patience, and to the quiet strength that drives human aspiration.

Over the years, I've had the privilege of listening to thousands of such voices. Some filled with excitement, some with hesitation, but all with hope. And in every one of them, I hear the heartbeat of why we exist.

Anita and Rajesh once came to us after years of frustration and false promises. Today, they run a small café in Toronto, their dream built on trust, not transaction. Ahmed, an entrepreneur from Dubai, had a complex, multi-jurisdictional case. What resolved it was not just expertise, but empathy, the ability to listen before acting.

Vikram, an engineer who migrated to Australia, told me that his son once said, "Your honesty paid off." That moment reminded me why we do what we do, because integrity, once practiced, becomes generational.

Meera, who chose Portugal for her golden visa investment, appreciated not the speed of our process, but the sincerity behind it. And Jonathan, a global mobility client, said what touched him most was that he always felt he was speaking to people, not a company.

In our 2024 client audit survey:

- 96% of clients described their experience as emotionally reassuring, proving that connection matters more than convenience.
- 91% said they would recommend our team because of integrity, not incentives.
- 87% cited transparent communication as the top reason for trust, the same value that shaped our foundation sixteen years ago.

As I look toward the next decade, I see the future of our team not as an expansion, but as an evolution, from a migration company to a movement of mindful migration. A future where every family feels empowered by knowledge, not pressured by fear. Where technology amplifies empathy, not replaces it. Where global mobility becomes a bridge built on transparency.

The true measure of success is not how many people we move across borders, but how many we move closer to their dreams.

Clients' Voices About the Future

SCAN ME

For most firms, the relationship with a client ends once the visa is granted. With us, that moment marks a new beginning. We stay in touch long after migration is complete, through follow-up calls, community programs, and an open-door policy that welcomes questions years after settlement. Our digital platforms connect clients from across the world, building a network of shared experience and support.

This approach has led to an extraordinary statistic:

Over 68 percent of new clients in 2024 came through referrals from previous clients. That single number says what words cannot, satisfaction becomes advocacy when trust is real.

The Spirit of Gratitude

Every letter, every message, and every reunion with clients reinforces our purpose. We celebrate their milestones as our own, when a student becomes a citizen, when an investor opens their first business abroad, or when a family sends back photos of their new home. Behind every smiling photograph lies a journey filled with courage and guided by care.

We often say that while policies shape migration, people shape meaning. Our clients give our work purpose, and their gratitude keeps our commitment unwavering. In the years ahead, migration systems will continue to change, but the essence of trust will remain timeless. Technology may simplify the process, but it will never replace the reassurance of human honesty.

The voices of our clients remind us that leadership in migration is not earned through volume or visibility, but through responsibility. Their stories are the living legacy of our team, a legacy built not on promises made, but on promises kept.

The future of migration will not be written by policies alone.

It will be written by people who lead with purpose, innovate with integrity, and protect with empathy. As the world grows smaller and movement grows smarter, our team will continue to stand where trust meets transformation, guiding families, professionals, and investors toward safer, brighter horizons.

Because progress may change form, but principles never go out of date.

Conclusion: A Vision Beyond Today

The future of migration is not a story of movement alone.

It is a story of courage, compassion, and connection. It is the story of humanity learning to coexist not as nations, but as neighbors.

In the years ahead, people will cross borders not only to find opportunity, but also to find belonging. Societies will continue to evolve as cultures intertwine, and economies will reshape themselves around shared values of cooperation and inclusion. The lines that divide maps will become less important than the bridges that unite hearts.

Migration will no longer be about documents or destinations. It will be about purpose. The purpose of creating a world where people can live where they grow, where talent is welcomed, and where trust defines every step of the journey.

For us, this vision is not a hope for tomorrow. It is a promise we live each day.

We do not see migration as a process. We see it as a transformation, a journey that changes both people and places.

Every file that comes to us carries a universe within it.

It holds a child who dreams of studying in a safer classroom.

It holds a professional who wishes to find dignity in honest work.

It holds a family that hopes to breathe easier, live freely, and create a future filled with stability and peace.

These are not case numbers. They are living stories that deserve care and protection.

We treat every journey as something sacred. Behind every policy we study and every application we guide lies a deeper understanding that our work touches lives and builds futures.

In a world that often moves too fast, we choose steadiness.

In an industry that often competes for attention, we choose compassion.

And in an age that constantly changes, we choose the consistency of truth and care.

Migration, for us, is not business. It is the work of humanity. It is the bridge that connects courage with opportunity and turns dreams into direction.

The Future Belongs to Responsibility

The next chapter of global mobility will be defined by one truth. Responsibility will be the new measure of strength.

The world is moving faster than ever before, but speed without sensitivity leads nowhere. Technology grows smarter each year, yet intelligence without empathy has no meaning. Progress in the years ahead will belong to those who combine innovation with integrity and growth with grace.

We are ready for that future.

Our systems will continue to ensure accuracy and foresight.

Our people will continue to bring compassion to every interaction.

Our leadership will always uphold ethics as the foundation of every success.

We do not measure achievement by the number of visas approved. We measure it by the number of lives made secure, the families reunited, and the dreams turned into reality.

The future of migration will not belong to those who promise the most. It will belong to those who protect the most.

A Responsibility That Transforms

Every generation inherits a challenge. Ours is to ensure that migration remains a force for good. It must uplift rather than divide. It must connect rather than exploit.

Through policy intelligence, collaboration, and empathy, our team continues to shape what responsible migration means. Each journey we facilitate contributes to something larger than itself: a stronger global community, a more inclusive world, and a shared legacy of trust.

Our mission continues with quiet purpose.

We exist not only to open doors, but to ensure that once opened, they stay open for generations to come.

The Light That Leads

Every story reaches its final page, yet some continue long after the book is closed.

The story of migration is one of those. It is renewed every time someone dares to begin again.

Migration, at its heart, is the desire for growth. It is the oldest human instinct, the belief that a better tomorrow exists just beyond the horizon. It is the faith that progress is possible when we have the courage to take the first step.

The work of our team honors that faith.

Every consultation, every policy interpretation, and every approval represents more than professional success. It represents a family placing its trust in us, believing that we will guide them with care and honesty.

We carry that trust as one carries light.

Light, when shared, does not fade. It multiplies.

The light of ethics becomes transparency.

The light of knowledge becomes empowerment.

The light of compassion becomes belonging.

Together, these lights form the legacy of our team, a legacy that shines wherever dreams cross borders.

The world will continue to change. Borders will shift. Laws will evolve. But as long as people continue to dream of better lives, there will always be a need for those who guide with integrity.

I promise that this name Varun Singh will remain that guide. Quietly. Faithfully. Responsibly. Turning migration into more than movement, and progress into something that truly endures.